The HEALING TREE

A MERMAID, A POET, AND A MIRACLE

JOE TYE

The Healing Tree
A Mermaid, a Poet, and a Miracle

This is a work of fiction and a product of the author's imagination. Any resemblance to real-world people, organizations, or events is strictly coincidental.

Published by Paradox 21 Press

Book Design and Illustration: Studio 6 Sense • studio6sense.com

ISBN#: 9781-887511-29-2

"I have heard the mermaids singing, each to each…

We have lingered in the chambers of the sea."

T.S. Eliot: *The Love Song of J. Alfred Prufrock*

PRAISE FOR THE HEALING TREE
(FROM THE ORIGINAL SELF-PUBLISHED EDITION)

"*The Healing Tree* is a book that you will not be able to put down... I started reading and was completely swept up in the spell-binding story! *The Healing Tree* is completely captivating, soul-enriching and beautifully written. I was blown away with the creativity, the brilliance and the talent of Joe Tye. Out of ALL of the books that I have read in my lifetime (and believe me I've read thousands of books), this is one of THE best books I have ever read. I love it, love it, love it. If you are ready to be emotionally moved in a beautiful way get a copy of The Healing Tree now (or get two copies and give one to someone you deeply care about)."

Peggy McColl, author of *Your Destiny Switch*
and *21 Distinctions of Wealth*

"Anyone facing a serious illness, either personally or with a loved one, should read *The Healing Tree*. This heart-warming story shows how a time of trial can become a time for hope, faith, self-discovery, and ultimate transcendence. This is a book for anyone seeking to find meaning in a time of adversity."

C. Everett Koop, M.D., Sc.D., author of
Koop: Memoirs of America's Family Doctor

"*The Healing Tree* is an inspirational book that lifts up all the important themes of pain, struggle, loss, hope, and renewal. Its life-affirming message of 'Yes You Can' is important for all of us, not just those in the healing professions."

James A. Autry, author of *Love and Profit* and *The Servant Leader*

"If you haven't believed in miracles, you will after reading *The Healing Tree*. In fact, you may go out and create your own miracles."

W Mitchell, author of *It's Not What Happens to You,
It's What You Do About It*

"*The Healing Tree* is an inspiring, touching account that will bring comfort to anyone facing life's most difficult decisions."

Larry Dossey, M.D., author of
Reinventing Medicine and Healing Words

"A delight to read. *The Healing Tree* takes you on an enlightening journey of self-discovery. This is a richly human book that will touch both your heart and mind."

Roger Crawford, author of *How High Can You Bounce?*

"*The Healing Tree* is a powerful reaffirmation of our real mission in the caring professions, and a poignant reminder that healing is a miraculous process which encompasses much more than just a physical cure. This book moved me to tears, but it also lifted my spirits and made me proud to be part of the movement to bring a greater sense of holistic healing into the traditional healthcare delivery system."

Patrick Charmel, co-author of *Putting Patients First*

"*The Healing Tree* is an inspiring story guaranteed to warm the hearts and souls of those who read it. Carrie Anne's path is indeed healing."

Brian Luke Seaward, Ph.D., author of *Quiet Mind, Fearless Heart*

"If the measure of a great book is its ability to be read and re-read over time and to have the experience grow deeper each time, then *The Healing Tree* passes the test with flying colors. With each new 'passage' in our lives, a re-reading of this book is in order, something that can be said of only a small number of books today."

Mike Casey, Professor of English, Graceland University

If you enjoyed

The Healing Tree

you will want to read

The Florence Prescription

Your Dreams Are Too Small

Never Fear, Never Quit

3 stories that can change your life.

These books and others can be purchased at
www.SparkStore.com

COMING NEXT:
LILIES IN THE SNOW

Life is a garden in the mountains, lovely and precarious. My father told me that the day I left for college 26 years ago. Now that the divorce had come through, I was happily tending to the garden of my new life. Before the Gray Lady confronted me in the violence of that liquid earthquake, it was a life where dead writers stayed dead and James MacWilder was just a photo on the back of a book jacket; a life where writing my own stories was something I would get around to — someday; a life where death was just the vague rumor of a distant catastrophe I wouldn't personally experience until long after I'd written the last of those stories. Enjoy the lilies as soon as they bloom, my father had said, because one morning you might wake up to find them covered with snow.

DEDICATION

For Doug, born with the heart of a musician
and the soul of a poet, who has always been a source
of amazement and inspiration to his Dad.

For Annie, who from that first toddle
over to the spring horse, has lived life as an adventure.

For Sally, because happiness is
being married to your best friend.

Contents

The greatest miracle of all is not
something that happens to you,
it's something that happens within you.
This is the story of one such miracle.

THE EIGHT BALL ROLLED TO A DEAD STOP *in front of the pool table's corner pocket and perched there like a fresh egg waiting for a short order cook to crack it open. Sammy DiMarco took a swig from his longneck Corona, set it down on the counter, and chalked up his custom pool cue. He walked slowly around the table, kissing the St. Pauli Girl poster for luck on the way, and positioned himself on the opposite end of the table from the money ball. Yes indeed, this was his night.*

"Deadeye." He repeated the affirmation to the rhythm of his breathing: Deadeye in, Deadeye out – Deadeye in, Deadeye out. "Words have power," his father had always told him, "so be careful what you call yourself." Sammy set the chalk down on the edge of the table and sprinkled baby powder on his left hand. Closing his eyes and taking a slow deep breath, he pushed out of his mind the memory of all the missed shots, of all those times he'd capped a brilliant run by choking on the money ball. Deadeye in, Deadeye out.

Sammy leaned over the table and peered across the seven feet of green felt that separated him from an easy two hundred bucks. He pumped his cue back and forth, slow and deliberate, and in his mind's eye visualized a taut crimson thread connecting the white cue ball with the black eight ball. The money ball. Slowly, Sammy pulled back the stick one last time, until his hand was parallel to the tobacco tin in the back pocket of his favorite denim jeans. The jukebox and the chatter of The Blue Room Bar faded into the shadows as he zeroed in. The instant the chalked tip of his stick punched into the cue ball, Sammy knew he'd won the game. The money ball slammed into the back of the corner pocket and disappeared down the rabbit hole.

After buying a round of drinks and giving the waitress an overgenerous tip, Sammy sauntered across the parking lot, oblivious to the cool night air and the full moon giving its benediction from above. The metal flake paint of his classic Dodge Charger sparkled candy apple red under the parking lot lights. He eased himself into the black leather bucket seat and slid the key into the ignition. Sammy pressed down on the polished aluminum accelerator pedal and the Charger's fuel-injected hemi roared in response. "Life is good," Sammy crooned as he rammed the chrome stick shift into first gear and gunned the Charger out of the parking lot.

Saturday night traffic was backed up all along Howard Street. As the Charger crawled past the First Guardian Bank building, Sammy looked over at the clock where time and temperature leapfrogged each other toward an invisible finish line. He cursed under his breath, then shuddered slightly, vaguely aware of having stirred a subterranean memory of the taste of soap which had been irrevocably linked to those words in the years before he ran away from home. He was an hour late, and Sheila was not a patient woman. "Time for a shortcut, Deadeye," he said aloud. Sammy zipped through the shopping mall parking lot and came out on Benson Boulevard.

"No lights, no law, no loitering."

As last words go, that pretty well captured all Sammy DiMarco had ever wanted out of life. He put the Charger through the gears, pressing himself back against the leather seat.

Just past the Galapagos Restaurant, Sammy had to slam on the brakes to avoid rear-ending an 18-wheeler wheezing its way up the hill. He downshifted and jammed the gas pedal to the floor as he yanked the Charger into the opposing lane to pass.

The last thing Deadeye DiMarco saw on this earth was the horrified faces of Mark and Carrie Anne Murphy the split second before they disappeared behind the airbags of their brand new Chevy Cavalier.

Chapter One

"WE'RE LOSING HER!"

The words caromed around inside my head like a housefly trapped in a Coke bottle. *We're losing her, losing her, losing her.* Such a commotion – the urgent voices and the clang-a-bang bustle. I hid behind my eye lids and followed the words as they rattled around in the darkness. *Weeeeee're loooooooosing herrrrrrrrrr!*

I must surely have been smiling and tapping my feet to the rhythm as the lyrics ricocheted from wall-to-wall in the attic of my mind. *We-we-we (Bop!) loo-loo-loo (Oh Yeah!) we-loo, we-loo, we-loo-loo-loo her (Oh No!).* But I couldn't tell. My body seemed somehow to have been misplaced. No tapping feet, no sing-along smile. Maybe they'd been lost, too, gone off with whoever it was those frantic people with the urgent voices were afraid of losing.

Curious now, I drifted up to the far corner of the room, free as a dandelion puff on a summer breeze. The room was awash in brilliant white light, making the people with the urgent voices stand out like the teeth in a toothpaste commercial. All clad in green and splotched with blood, they hovered over the broken lady who was lying on a narrow gurney in the middle of the room. The broken lady was white, too, but more like the white of curdled milk.

How funny. The broken lady was right there in the middle of the room where those frantic people in their bloody green scrubs could see her and touch her, and still they were losing her. *We-we-we (Bop!) loo-loo-loo (Oh No!)*.

Looking down from my perch up in the corner near the ceiling, I gradually began to comprehend why I couldn't tap my feet or put on my smile. The broken lady had them.

The broken lady never did give me back my feet. And she kept my smile for a very long time. She might never have given that back either had it not been for the miracle of Maggie. Maggie Mermaid and the healing tree.

SWITCH

With the simple flip of a cosmic switch
your life descends into a darkness
that not even the sun can penetrate.
Who flipped that switch
you may never know.

Only one hand can bring back the light.
But that hand must first
find its way to the switch
through the shadows.

That hand will need a guide.

Carrie Anne Murphy

Chapter Two

The month after the accident was pretty eventful. My husband Mark was buried. My son Robbie moved in with one of our neighbors. Mark's brother Randy came up from Dallas to deal with the doctors, the lawyers and the insurance companies. I guess there were quite a few important decisions to be made. I slept through it all.

The doctors later told me I was lucky to have survived, though it would be a long time before I joined them in that judgment. The police estimated that the drunk driver who rammed into us was going at least 70. With our combined speeds, they said it was like running into a brick wall at over 100 miles per hour. That image of crashing into an unyielding brick wall would haunt my dreams for the rest of my life. Mark's neck was fractured when his head bounced off the airbag and into the Cavalier's ceiling before slamming into the side window. He died instantly, they told me.

In the split second during which Mark was dying, the passenger's side airbag exploded from its cocoon behind the dash, and while that prevented me from flying into the windshield (or, more accurately, prevented the windshield from flying into me), it also fractured my nose and knocked out my front teeth. The drunk was driving a bigger car, and going a lot faster. At the moment of impact, his souped-up motor crashed into the space occupied by the much smaller engine of our Cavalier, forcing it back into the passenger compartment. This caused the frame to buckle upward and backward at the same time my momentum was carrying me forward and downward.

In a panicked reaction just before the collision, I'd braced my legs against the floorboard. Both legs were shattered in more places than the radiologists could count. As my legs were being crushed against my hips, my upper body was reeling from the violent impact with the airbag. Something had to give, and what gave was my lower spine. Two vertebrae were fractured and the spinal cord was crunched.

The punk hot rodder wasn't wearing a seatbelt. He crashed through the windshield of his car, and apparently did a somersault across the roof of ours before hitting the pavement some twenty or so yards beyond the point of the crash.

He was also killed instantly, they said. Except in the dark world of my fantasies, where he lived long enough to be castrated and mutilated, flogged and keelhauled, then stretched and broken on the rack and burned at the stake before being turned over to the mercies of the master of the underworld. It took a long time, but I eventually came to appreciate just how toxic and malignant was the hatred I'd harbored for so long for that dead stranger who had killed my husband and broken my body. As it turned out, planting that hatred under the shade of the healing tree was as much a part of my healing as the medical treatment. First I had to hang on, then I had to let go.

Breaking the News

Turn off the television, stow the paper away.
Let talk radio talk to someone else tonight.
Send the gossips out for more coffee.
Shut the door.
Just you and me – alone in this quiet room.
It's time for the evening news.

C.A.M.

Chapter Three

This should hurt. That was the first thought I had when I woke up. Somehow, even then, at the first dawning of my new existence, I knew that the absence of pain was not a good thing.

The sky above was filled with fluffy white clouds, but the clouds were not moving. Neither were the birds silhouetted against the unnaturally blue sky. Something else amiss here. *Where am I?* A surge of panic started in my belly and worked its way up toward my lungs. It stuck in my throat when I tried to scream. I closed my eyes and a chaotic montage of memories flashed through my consciousness. Robbie standing at the front door waving goodbye. That sudden blinding light. Trying to put my hands in front of my face, yet instinctively knowing it would be too late. Strobing red lights puncturing the nightmare darkness. Screaming voices, close by but incomprehensible, like listening to foreigners shouting at each other in a subway station. Man with a flashlight crawling in through the windshield, holding my face in his hands. Looking down from my serene corner at the broken lady and the frantic people in their bloody green scrubs. *We're losing her!* echoing in my brain. Then, nothing.

I think a long time must have passed before I opened my eyes again. The clouds had not moved, and the unflying birds were still frozen in the fake sky. The rest of the room gradually began to come into focus. The clouds and the birds weren't moving because they were painted on the ceiling. Off to my right side, I heard the soft beeping of some sort of machine. *Where am I?*

I tried to turn my head toward the noise and discovered that I *could* still feel pain. It felt like someone had run a hot iron from my neck down to my waist. My throat finally released its death grip on my vocal chords and something came out, but it hardly sounded human. More like the croak of an indignant raven. I tried to sit up, but was rewarded only by a spastic flailing of one arm in front of my face.

To my left, I heard a loud crash. Without thinking, I twisted my head in that direction and suffered another jolt of searing pain. I closed my eyes and croaked again, the noise vibrating against the sandpaper dryness of my throat. I squinted my eyes open. Someone was standing there. A woman dressed in white. Her hand was over her mouth, her eyes wide.

Another woman in white hurried into the room. She looked down at the spilled tray on the floor, then over at me. Now she covered her mouth. "Oh my God. She's awake." I closed my eyes and drifted back into the velvet darkness.

When I woke up again, I was surrounded by people in white. They were all busy, fussing over me. The broken lady. *Oh No!*

"Mark?" I couldn't make his name come out past the sandpaper in my throat. I tried again. "Mark?" Everyone stopped what they were doing and looked at the tall man in the long white coat standing next to my shoulder. I recognized the stethoscope draped around his neck as the latest model of a very ancient talisman: he was a medicine man. He pinched his chin between his thumb and forefinger and stared at me for a very long minute. Then he looked around and said, "Give us a few minutes here." Everyone else filed quietly out of the room and I sensed the door whispering shut behind them.

The man in the long white coat turned off the beeping of the machine, then sat on the edge of the bed and put his hand on my forearm. He looked vaguely familiar. "Mrs. Murphy?" I blinked, and that seemed to be sufficient acknowledgment for him to proceed. "I'm Dr. Paulson, chief trauma surgeon here at Memorial Hospital." Now I remembered where I'd seen him before. *We're losing her!* I closed my eyes, wishing that I'd stayed up in that high corner and not allowed them to drag me back into the broken lady's body. "Mark?" I mouthed his name again.

Dr. Paulson didn't answer at once. He looked out the window, then back at me. His hand was still on my forearm. "When people ask what keeps me in medicine, with all the long hours, hard work and bureaucratic hassles," he finally said, "I tell them that I get strength from my patients, from people who must bear the unbearable and yet still find a way to go on. People who make the choice to go on, when it would be easy for them to quit. If I'm not mistaken, Carrie Anne, you've already made that choice once."

Closing my eyes again, my thoughts drifted back to that moment when I first looked down upon the broken lady. Yes, I knew even then – the pain was going to be unbearable. And still, I had chosen to come back.

"You know you're in the hospital?" I nodded – very slightly, for fear of bringing back that blistering pain. Dr. Paulson looked at me like he was trying to see what was on the inside of my skin. "You've been here for almost five weeks." He let that sink in, and I knew that worse was still to come. He shifted his weight on the bed, picked up my hand and held it in both of his, gently rubbing my palm with his thumbs. *How do they teach this in medical school? Breaking the News 101.*

"You were in an accident... Both your legs were severely fractured." His eyes never left mine. "Your back was also broken. When you've regained your strength, the orthopedic docs will have to do more surgery, put in some pins and rods." A picture of the broken lady came back to me, and in the image I saw something I hadn't noticed before. She had a big foam collar around her neck, and was strapped onto a long wooden board. Dr. Paulson nodded, as if to say, *Yes, Carrie Anne, you are the broken lady, and I'm afraid you're broken beyond repair.* Then he simply said, "it will be a while before we can know for certain, but I'm afraid that right now it looks like you might not walk again." *We-we-we (bop!) loo-loo-loo (Oh No!).*

"Mark?" I again mouthed my husband's name. I already knew the answer. And I knew that Dr. Paulson had been wrong about me. I did not have the strength to bear this pain. Except this time I would not have a choice.

"It was a head-on collision. It probably happened so fast that Mark never even saw the other car coming. I'm sorry." At that moment I needed to be hugged more than I needed my next breath of air, but Dr. Paulson couldn't have made it past all the tubes and wires even if he'd tried. He set down my hand, stood up from the bed, and used a washcloth on my cheeks. "You need to cry, Carrie Anne, but I need to keep your stitches dry," he said with a gentle smile. It was only later that I learned my nose had been broken and my facial lacerations had required more than 100 stitches, something he had considered hardly worth mentioning after all I'd just learned.

"Robbie?" Once more, no sound came out, but thankfully Dr. Paulson was adept at lip-reading. "He's been here every day. He's at school right now. Maggie will pick him up and bring him by this afternoon. Robbie is quite a young man, very mature for a 15-year-old. Told me he's thinking about medical school. I hope you don't mind, but I encouraged him. He'd make a fine doctor."

Dr. Paulson looked at the clock on the wall, then back at me. "It's not quite noon, and Maggie will be bringing Robbie in at about four, so why don't you close your eyes for a while. We're pumping some high-powered painkillers into you, and you've had a pretty rough morning."

I wanted desperately to lose myself behind a veil of sleep, but even more desperately wanted for it to already be afternoon so I could see my son, who evidently had made a new friend. "Maggie?"

Dr. Paulson smiled almost all the way into a laugh. "Maggie Mermaid is the hospital's poetry therapist. She's sort of taken Robbie under her wing, appointed herself his official chauffer.

You'll meet her before long. If you're a patient at Memorial Hospital, you can't escape meeting Maggie."

I closed my eyes and drifted back into the void, into a dream I was to have many times more in the months to come. I was back up in my serene little corner, looking down on all the those frantic people in their bloody green scrubs as they scurried around the broken lady. The room grew suddenly hushed, and Mark walked in flashing the big smile that had once so infatuated an insecure and lonely teenage girl. Everyone stepped aside to clear a path for him. He bent over the broken lady and kissed her on the lips. Then he wrapped his arms around her and lifted her up from the gurney. He gently set her down on the floor, and just like that the foam collar fell from her neck and all the tubes and wires dropped to the ground. No longer broken, she walked out of the room, hand-in-hand with Mark.

The doctors and nurses in the bloody green scrub suits were astonished. All the broken lady had really needed was a hug.

INCONVENIENCED

"They say it's two miles long" says the man
in the stained denim work shirt and aviator sunglasses
as he holsters his cell phone and glares furiously
at the smoldering parking lot snaking its way across
the landscape where just 15 minutes earlier
there had been a living breathing highway.

"God, I can't believe it," says the man from the BMW
who has slung his jacket over his shoulder and
loosened his tie so as to allow the profanities
smoother passage toward the ears of fellow bystanders,
"only the DOT could create a mess like this."

"Your tax dollars at work," says the man
with the three-day old beard
leaning out the window of his beat-up red pickup truck
who doesn't really seem to be in much of a hurry
to get anywhere anyway.

The young woman in the blue blazer, awkward in her heels,
Walks over from the brown Civic, looks twice at her watch.
"I'll miss my job interview," she says, and you
can't tell if she's trying to hold back tears
of anger and frustration
or tears of relief.

Several days later they each again drive by

that spot two miles on down the highway

but no one seems to notice

the tiny cross of flowers

that has sprouted up

in the grass

on the little hill

by the roadside.

C.A.M

As it turned out, I didn't see Robbie that afternoon after all. I slept through another visit. That was probably a good thing. While I don't think I could have survived without morphine helping me hide from the pain, the drug reduced my conversational aptitude to that of a drunken parrot. Though I didn't see him that day, Robbie was very much in my dreams.

Shortly before Mark and I had left for dinner on our last night together, I'd suggested bringing Robbie along. Mark, ever the hopeless romantic, replied that intimate candlelight dinners and 15-year-old boys were mutually exclusive, and that in any event Robbie would rather be home with pizza and video games. In the chaos of my nightmare universe, though, Robbie somehow kept showing up in the backseat of the Cavalier. At the moment of impact, I would reach out to grab him as he went hurtling toward the windshield, but he'd always slip through my fingers. "Bye, Mom," I'd hear him say as he disintegrated into the maelstrom of flying glass and twisted metal. Then everything would go black.

"Hi, Mom." It was a Saturday, seven weeks after the accident. A red letter day. They'd just elevated the back of my bed so that for the first time since the accident I could be in a semi-sitting position instead lying of flat on my back. And they'd reduced my morphine dosage, so it was the first time I was really awake for the visit of my son.

They hadn't let me look in a mirror yet (not that I'd have wanted to), and Robbie did an admirable job of pretending that his mother didn't look like a used Halloween mask. Seven weeks ago we'd left a boy at home with the promise that we'd be back before his bedtime. Today, a young man was telling me how he and his uncle were remodeling the house to make it wheelchair accessible, and about the decisions they'd made on my behalf. "And get this, Mom, Mrs. Marchant even taught me how to iron a shirt." Cheri Marchant was our next-door neighbor.

"You can iron your own shirts?" I'd never really wanted him to grow out of diapers, and now here he was ironing his own shirts. I tried to concentrate as Robbie talked about insurance policies, legal papers, and loose ends at the bank, but mostly seeing him just made me think of how badly I missed Mark and how much I hated the man who had killed him. "There's one thing Uncle Randy and I agree on," Robbie said, crossing his arms the way Mark always used to do when he was about to draw some sort of line in the sand, "but you're not going to like it."

Mark's baby brother had, shall we say, a bit of a rebellious streak. At 38, he still rode his overgrown motorcycle down the highway without a helmet, wore one of those silly black leather vests all bedecked with patches from places he'd probably never been, and would soon be eligible to retire from the only job he'd ever held – sorting mail the post office. I braced myself for the news that my darling boy had decided to get a tattoo and run off with Uncle Randy to join a motorcycle gang. "What's that, Robbie?"

"The lawyer gave us a copy of your living will. It says that the doctors aren't supposed to do everything they can if you... You know, if you get in trouble."

"You mean more trouble." It was actually a relief that it was me, and not Robbie, we were talking about getting into trouble.

Robbie looked at me sternly. "Yeah. We're not willing to give up on you, and we don't think you should ever give up on yourself. No matter what." *Just like his father.*

What do you say to a boy who's already lost so much and is desperately trying to hold on to what's left? "They have wonderful doctors here, Robbie, and they're taking really good care of me. I'm going to be fine. So you guys don't need to worry about it." In the years to come, I would become a pro in the art of protective denial, but this early I'm afraid I didn't sound very convincing.

Robbie frowned. "What's the but? I can always tell when you're going to tack a 'but' onto what you just said." There was defiance in his eyes and he was obviously bracing himself to be the winner in a winner-take-all debate. *Just like Mark.*

"But you have to respect my wishes about this, Robbie. If things really get bad..." *Don't cry, Carrie Anne. Be strong for your son.* "If things really get bad, I want to be the mother you always remember, not the burden you come to resent." Robbie was about to protest, but I cut him off. "We don't need to settle this right now, but I'll make you a deal." Robbie was big on deals.

"What deal?"

"They don't think I'll ever walk again. I'll always be in a wheelchair. I can live with that. Lots of people do."

"So what's the deal?"

"I'd rather die than have them keep my body breathing when my brain is dead. That's not living, it's just existing, like a head of lettuce in the garden. If it gets to that point, Robbie, you have to let me go. Dad will be waiting for me, and you have to let me go."

Robbie's eyes welled with tears. *Just like his mother.* He blinked hard and put on his tough guy face. "So what's the deal? You said you'd make me a deal."

"If it comes to that... I don't believe it will, but if it comes to that, you and Uncle Randy talk to Dr. Paulson. You ask him to be precisely honest with you about what my prospects are. Then you put yourselves in my place. If you wouldn't want to live that way, like a plant out in the vegetable garden, then you have let me go. But if I have a fighting chance of having a real life – a real life, mind you, more than just having machines feed me and make me breathe while I take up a bed – then we'll make a fight of it. Deal?"

Robbie stood there with his arms crossed and his tough guy face screwed firmly in place.

"Deal?" I asked again, extending my right hand. Finally, the tough guy face softened and Robbie gently laid his hand into mine. "Deal."

That was to be the first of many such discussions, and of many such deals. There was the discussion, and the deal, when Robbie thought I was taking too much morphine; the discussion, and the deal, when I wanted to cut back on the visiting nurse service because I thought it was getting too expensive; the discussion, and the deal, when Robbie was going to apply to the local community college so he could be near me, and I insisted he attend a university that would prepare him to pursue his dream of medical school. So many discussions. So many deals.

"So," I said, anxious to change the subject. "Tell me about Maggie." Robbie shrugged in the manner of a teenage boy still pretending he hasn't yet discovered girls. "Is she cute?"

Robbie shrugged again. "She's old."

"Oh." For some reason I'd assumed Maggie would be a vivacious teenager. "How old is she?"

Another shrug. "I don't know. Twenty-five. Something like that."

"Oh. That is old. But is she cute?"

Robbie frowned and shook his head. "Not my type." It was news to me that Robbie had a type. "Besides, she has cancer."

"Oh no! I'm sorry to hear that." I don't know what I was expecting. Ever since Dr. Paulson had first mentioned Maggie the mermaid poet, I'd been creating a mental image of someone exotic and mysterious, a creature who looked like she'd just come down from the prow of a pirate ship to join Will Shakespeare and Ben Johnson at the pub. Now she turned out to be, at least in Robbie's eyes, an old lady with cancer. "Well, Dr. Paulson told me she's a poet. Has she written a poem for you?"

"No. But she said she's working on one for you. I told her you like poetry."

"What makes you think I like poetry?"

"When Uncle Randy and I were going through the attic, we found three boxes full of poetry books. They were all marked up and highlighted and stuff, like you were studying. So I figured you must like it."

I closed my eyes for a moment and fought off a flood of old memories. "Yeah, but it was more of a love-hate relationship."

"Well, anyway, I thought you might like something to read, so I brought a couple of them." Robbie pointed to a small pile of books on my bedside table. "In case you get tired of watching TV or something."

I didn't turn the TV on after Robbie left. Instead, next time the nurse's aide stopped by I asked her to choose a poetry book for me to read. She examined the covers, then laid one on my lap. "Looks like this one must be your favorite," she said as she raised the back of my bed a bit further so I could read, "the way all the pages been folded down like that."

I thanked her, then waited until she'd left to pick up the book. I already knew which book she'd selected; the one I'd read so many times that virtually every page was dog-eared. But shortly before Robbie was born, I'd quit reading poetry. Every poem was just another painful reminder that in the ninth grade I had disowned a part of myself. My poetry books had all been interred in a box in the attic. Only now, they'd been resurrected by my well-meaning son. I brushed away a fine film of dust from the book on my lap and read the bold type announcing what was inside:

RAGING SOULS
Poems by Angry Women

I knew that if I opened those covers, I might fall in and never climb back out. But I couldn't stop. Like Eve eyeing the most tempting apple in the garden, like Pandora running greedy fingers across the top of the forbidden box, I was being inexorably pulled down into the vortex of that awful book, back into the sisterhood of those luminous women whose acceptance, whose companionship, whose love, I had once desired as nothing else.

I wandered through the pages of *Raging Souls* in the manner of a grown-up returned to the neighborhood of her youth, seeing old and once-familiar places with new and wiser eyes, at one turn wondering how a verse that in memory was ornate and enchanting now seemed plain and quotidian, and beyond the next turn marveling at the subtle power of passages once dismissed the way a child bent upon getting to the playground would pass by a shoppe filled with ancient books and manuscripts. Once again, I climbed onto the emotional roller coaster I'd first ridden while hidden away in the closet of my childhood bedroom: the myth of virginity and the reality of rape; loving life while longing for death; angry at the god I refused to believe in. And as I stepped back onto that roller coaster, I knew this time the ride would be more violent.

Old poems took on new meanings as I meandered through the pages. I was in no hurry to reach the one that had been the source of so many nightmares – also knew I would have no choice but to go there. *The Death Baby.* Anne Sexton's ominous canto. I read the first two lines: *I was an ice baby. I turned to sky blue.*

Anne Sexton, the lonely poet who turned herself into an ice baby by sticking her head in the oven and turning on the gas. And now, Anne's nightmare had become my reality. From the wreckage of that accident, I had emerged reborn as the ice baby. Like a glacier flowing inexorably from the mountains, anger and hatred, grief and despair, encased my heart in a shroud of blue ice that not even my son's smile could penetrate. *I died seven times /*

in seven ways / letting death give me a sign / letting death place his mark on my forehead.

I closed the book and allowed myself a good cry. After a while, I opened it again to a page near the back, a neighborhood I hadn't really explored before packing the book away in the attic. My eyes went right to an untitled poem by Anna Akhmatova, that indomitable Russian woman who had endured so much tragedy and written such beautiful poems in the face of it all. I was caught fast by the opening line: *As I die, I long for immortality.* I read the final stanza six times:

> *The deadly hour will offer me*
> *Poison to drink – I won't have a choice*
> *People will come, and help to bury*
> *Both my body and my voice.*

The deadly hour. The hour surrounding that accident would forevermore be the great divide in my life. For 30 minutes, Mark and I held hands and called each other pet names that had grown more tender since high school, shared secrets known only to us as we headed toward our deadly rendezvous with that punk hot rodder. For 30 minutes, the ambulance crew cut through the wreckage of the car we'd only just bought with an eye toward Robbie's sixteenth birthday. And separating those two 30 minute fragments of my life was the flick of some cosmic switch, that incomprehensibly tiny fraction of a second that separated life before and life after as absolutely as a mountain chain divides a continent. I hit the IV button to give myself another dose of morphine and cried myself to sleep.

I knew I'd slept for several hours, because when I woke up the sun was setting outside the window of my hospital room. I opened *Raging Souls* to the very back, to the once-blank pages that were now covered with the smudged teenage musing of the girl that once was me. There was one small space remaining to be filled on the very last page, like the far corner of an old cemetery that would admit of only one or two more corpses before someone erected the "no vacancy" sign. Without consciously thinking, I picked up a pen from the bedside table and watched my hand push it across the paper.

In the sterile quiet of the exam room
doctor ponders the unusual x-ray.
What do you prescribe for chest pain
caused by a dying dream
trapped inside the heart?

I closed the book and laid it aside. It wasn't only my body that was broken; there was a dream dying in my heart, a dream that might soon be buried before it could be reborn. My heart raced and I could barely catch my breath. It was as if a dark black cloud had dropped from the sky and enveloped me with a hideous freezing evil. Was I about to run out of time? Poetry had always been something I would do later, only now it looked like later might come a whole lot sooner than I'd ever imagined. Though I had no way of knowing it at the time, the accident that destroyed my body – the poison I had to drink – was also the first step toward helping me find my voice.

MY APPLICATION TO JOIN THE DEAD POETS SOCIETY

I've sometimes been dead right
More often been dead wrong
I've have been fatally attracted
And sung a funeral song

I've tried to be dead serious
More than once I've been dead broke
I've swum with killer whales
And heard some killer jokes

I'm sometimes dead in the water
Other times dead on my feet
I've driven down many a dead end
Run in many a dead heat

I've been dead drunk, though long ago
They say I was white as a ghost
I've been locked in mortal combat
Survived a killing frost

I've sent my share of dead letters
Missed my share of dead lines
I've driven through Death Valley
Slept in an old ghost mine

In the dead of deep black night
I've laid in fear's dread tomb
In the dead of deep white winter
I've known the stillborn womb

I've seen the dead leaves falling

From branches of dying trees

But the vision of my own death mask

Scares the hell out of me

C.A.M.

Chapter Five

You know the feeling you get when you're sitting in your car at a stoplight, eyes straight ahead, minding your own business, and you can somehow tell the person in the adjacent car is staring at you? That's what it was like the first time I met Maggie. I'd been lying in my hospital bed staring at the clouds that never moved and the birds that didn't fly, wondering if Mark was really up there somewhere beyond that fake sky, waiting for me to come to him. Her voice came to me as a whisper in the woods.

"Would you like to hear your poem?"

Who knows how long she'd been standing there at my bedside waiting for the right moment to ask me that question. Gingerly turning my head to the left, I tried to make my eyes refocus. She was thin as a darning needle and had the wildest mane of red hair I'd ever seen outside of the zoo or a Dr. Seuss book. A scarlet-capped dandelion with mint green eyes and the smile of a two-year-old who's just been given a chocolate ice cream cone. I squinted to see what was written on her T-shirt. *When was the last time you did something for the first time?* Looking at Maggie, I got the impression it was a struggle for her to stand in one place without vibrating, and that the last time she'd done something for the first time was about five minutes ago. "My poem?"

"Yeah. It's one of the benefits of being a patient at Memorial Hospital. Room service poetry readings." She opened the pink journal that had been tucked under her arm and held it in front of her, like one of those carolers you see in the Christmas pictures, and smiled expectantly.

"So, you must be Maggie." I stated the obvious.

Maggie flushed crimson and put her hand over her mouth, then touched my arm. "Oh, I'm sorry! I should have introduced myself. I've been here so many times – but you were always asleep." She laughed and her eyes sparkled and the room must have warmed up by ten degrees. "Yeah, I'm Maggie. I'm one of the volunteers here. I specialize in writing poems for patients." She gave me a conspiratorial wink. "That's why I can get away with not wearing one of those stuffy volunteer uniforms – they *expect* poets to be weird, you know."

I shrugged. "I've never met a volunteer poet before. So I guess I wouldn't know."

Maggie laughed again. "Oh, I'm not just a poet." She leaned closer and half-whispered, "I'm also a mermaid."

"A mermaid!" I didn't know whether to laugh or press the nurse call button, since the obvious option of running away was not open to me.

"Yes," she replied, evidently pleased with having elicited the desired reaction. "You know how mermaids rescue drowning sailors?"

I nodded, even though it was news to me that mermaids rescued drowning sailors. "Well," she continued, "I rescue drowning souls."

"You rescue drowning souls?"

"Yeah. There are lots of people drowning here in the hospital. Drowning in pain and despair, drowning in hopelessness and self-pity. My poems are life preservers for drowning souls. Just a little something they can hang onto, something to keep them from sinking. You know, until they can swim on their own again." Maggie looked down into the pages of her pink journal, then back at me. "Do you want to hear your poem?" She said it as though meeting a real live mermaid in your hospital room was no big deal.

I nodded. "Sure, Maggie. I'd love to hear my poem."

She smiled, closed her eyes for a second composing herself. "It's called Invisible Wings." She cleared her throat and tried, unsuccessfully, to look serious. Then she read:

INVISIBLE WINGS

Make welcome the unwelcome guest.
Let her in through the hole in your heart.
Let go for a time what you cannot control.
Trust in God's time a new path will unfold.

   When you're lost in the waves
   you can't see the beach;
   when your soul has been splintered
   help seems beyond reach.

So open your heart to the terror and madness.
Give new wounds time to become ancient scars.
Sing to yourself the song of your sadness, and
share with new friends the voice of your hope.

   The snow in the mountains
   will melt in the spring;
   and angels on earth fly
   with invisible wings.

Maggie slowly closed her pink journal, without looking up at me. A memory flashed back, something I had not thought about in years and years. I was standing at the front of the room in my ninth grade English class. I'd just recited the poem we'd all had to compose as a homework assignment. I don't know what I was expecting when I'd finished. Fireworks and clanging church bells, maybe, or for God to come out of the whirlwind and congratulate me on my brilliance. Instead, it was the voice of Mr. Brightwood. *Thank you, Carrie Anne. Who wants to go next?* That's what I got instead of church bells and whirlwinds. I never wrote another poem.

I looked at this visiting mermaid poet through tear-filled eyes. At the time, I didn't know if I was crying for Maggie, who wore her heart on her sleeve, or if I was crying for little Carrie Anne, who had buried her heart underneath the linoleum floor of Mr. Brightwood's English classroom. It was only much later that I realized what Maggie had foreseen in her poem: losing my legs meant that I had to stop running away from a dream that had been chasing me since the ninth grade.

Chapter Six

My son is a genius. While I was sleeping off the world's most gargantuan hangover, Robbie had gone through old scrapbooks, shoeboxes full of unsorted photos, and hundreds of videos, put it all together in a *Greatest Hits of Mark and Carrie Anne Murphy* movie, then loaded it onto a laptop computer for me. Mark and Carrie Anne hauling their backpacks through the Rockies; Mark and Carrie Anne picnicking under giant redwood trees; Mark and Carrie Anne hiking in the Grand Canyon; Mark and Carrie Anne cruising along the vibrant reefs of Cozumel. Mark and Carrie Anne carrying on for the little man who after so many years of prayerful waiting had finally become a part of our family. Mark and Carrie Anne doing the things together that Carrie Anne would never be able to do alone.

I'd been watching the movie all morning, sitting in bed with the laptop floating weightlessly on my thighs. It's funny how things that seem insignificant at the time later emerge as magnitudinous markers of an impending change perhaps known to God but as-yet unseen by those of us on earth. In the last vignette of Robbie's montage, I was videotaping Mark and Robbie as they strapped on their bicycle helmets, something they had done every Saturday morning for years. In the background were the three new bikes Mark bought after he'd gotten a raise – five weeks before the accident. The end was coming soon, I knew. Two of the bikes had already been sent to the Goodwill. From this point on, our movie would be filled only with partings, funerals, and sorrow.

There was a soft knock on the door. "Can I come in?" It was Maggie.

I turned off the computer and folded down the top. "Sure, Maggie. Are you out making your poetry rounds?"

Maggie took a tentative step into the room. "Sort of. Well, actually, it's not just me." She looked back out into the hallway and waved for whoever was out there to come in. "This goes against the wall, under the clock," she said, pointing to the space opposite the foot of my bed. Two men wearing uniforms of the hospital maintenance department came in pushing a 40-gallon aquarium that was mounted on some sort of stand with wheels. While one of them polished the glass, the other fiddled around with the plugs and filters. In no time it was bubbling a happy song.

"Perfect," Maggie exclaimed as she admired the aquarium. It *was* beautiful – a saltwater tank populated by creatures that God must have created while in her most jovial mood. Maggie peered into the tank, pointed at something floating inside and said, "That's my favorite!" It was a petite pink plastic mermaid, blowing bubbles as she glided through her cozy little home under the indoor sea.

"Okay," said Maggie, putting her hands on her hips, "that takes care of the ocean. Now, the mountain goes over here." She removed the towels and the blue plastic water pitcher from my bedside cabinet. The two maintenance guys went back out into the corridor, and returned pushing an aluminum utility cart with a squeaky wheel.

The cart carried a wooden board that had been covered with green felt, and apparently cut to be just the right size to fit atop my bedside cabinet. There was a miniature papier-mâché mountain standing at one corner. A little blue stream had been painted coming down from the mountain and flowing across the green felt field. A minuscule gravel path, complete with tiny cairns to mark the trail, traversed the green field toward the mountain. Maggie admired the wilderness scene, looking like a little kid who's just found the biggest, most colorful egg on Easter morning. Then she went over to the corner and pushed the visitor chair (the one that Mark should have been sitting in) to the side. "Okay, guys, the tree goes here."

"The tree?" Maggie disappeared through the door without answering me. About ten minutes later, she and the guys from maintenance came back pushing a big cart with a tree on it. A real live tree. A 3-foot tall sycamore tree planted in a pot that was painted to look like a flower garden. The maintenance guys strained to lift the pot and place it on the floor as Maggie chirped directions. "No, no – over just a few inches. She needs to get the afternoon sun, you know."

The maintenance guys left without even looking in my direction – another reminder of how hard people try to avoid contact with ugly people, and how ugly I must still be, with my missing teeth and twisted nose and as-yet unhealed scars. Not to mention the worthless appendages buried under the hospital sheets. One of the first things they teach you when you learn to ski is how to drive your edges into the snow to bring yourself to a stop. That had become my metaphor for trying to stop myself from sliding down the black ice slope of depression. I'd envision myself schussing along and then, with the grace of an Olympic medal winner, throwing up a plume of emotional snow as I skidded to a stop. Sometimes it actually worked, and thankfully this was one of those times. "Why, Maggie, this is all really beautiful. Thank you."

Maggie beamed. "I figured if Carrie Anne can't go to the mountains and the ocean, and out to the hospital healing garden, then we should bring the mountains and the ocean, and the healing garden, to Carrie Anne."

"I love it all Maggie, especially the tree. I've really missed seeing trees."

Maggie stepped over to the tree and picked a shriveled leaf off one of the branches. "This is a very special tree. This is the healing tree. She's full of mystical healing powers, you know."

Maggie leaned in and took a deep breath, as if simply sharing the tree's air would make her cancer go away. "Can't you just feel her magic?"

"She is a beautiful tree, Maggie, but I'm afraid there's no magic in the world to heal what's wrong with me." *Or you.* I didn't say those two words out loud, but the instant they popped into my head they rang of certainty, the sort of bleak inevitability you would imagine a bug feeling under the shadow of a shoe, and self-pity was joined by guilt as I resumed the slide down that icy emotional slope.

Maggie let down the bedrail and sat on the side of my bed. "I'm really sorry about all the bad stuff that's happened to you, Carrie Anne. But don't lose hope. Miracles do happen, you know. Maybe the healing tree's magic really will help."

"Yeah, I'm sorry too. We're all sorry, aren't we?" The darkness was closing round again. "You know, Maggie, I'm sick to death of hearing that word sorry. Aren't you? Don't you get tired of people looking at you with pity in their eyes? I know I do."

Maggie scrunched her face like a child who'd just been given her first taste of kiwi fruit and was trying to decide which "ish" it was: delicious or atrocious. Then she said, "Where there is beauty, there must also be pity, for the very reason that beauty must die. Vladimir Nabokov said that. So every time somebody looks at me with pity, I just assume they're really trying to tell me I'm beautiful, and I thank them! Try it – it will give you a whole new perspective."

"Well, there's a connection missing somewhere, Maggie, because for all the self-pity I have, I sure don't feel beautiful. Did you see the way those two maintenance guys tried to pretend I wasn't even in the room?"

Maggie leaned over and kissed me on the forehead. "Don't think of beautiful as an adjective, Carrie Anne. Think of it as a noun. Beautiful is not what you look like, it's who you are. Real beauty is what's reflected from the inside looking out, not what's seen from the outside looking in."

In my dreams after Maggie had left, I sat on a swing suspended from a branch of the healing tree. Mark and Robbie waved to me from the top of the mountain at the end of the trail. They were waiting for me to hop off the swing and hike up the trail to join them. My wheelchair was parked by the edge of the stream, where it made a fine perch for the birds and butterflies. And I was beautiful.

Chapter Seven

"How'd you sleep last night, Carrie Anne?" Dr. Paulson was the undoctor – he always started out by asking human questions, and only after he'd processed the answers did he move on to medical matters. I nodded and smiled. It hurt too much to talk, but I'd actually slept well for the first time since the latest surgery. Over the past three months, the orthopedic surgeons had operated on both legs twice and on my back once, the plastic surgeon had tried to hide the scars, the oral surgeon had screwed in new front teeth, and now I was recovering from having had my appendix taken out. (Gawd, can you believe it! My appendix! As if I hadn't already done my share to keep the operating room nurses fully employed.) I let my imagination take me on a stroll through the forest I pictured surrounding the healing tree while Dr. Paulson read through the nurse's notes. He closed the chart at last and laid it on the bed next to me. "What do you think," he asked, "are you ready for some real food?"

Before I could answer (the answer would have been no), Maggie erupted into the room with a cackle. "Did I hear someone say food?"

Dr. Paulson rolled his eyes with mock exasperation. "Maggie, do the words 'do not disturb' mean anything to you?"

Maggie shot a quizzical glance at Dr. Paulson, then smiled and winked at me. "You mean, like those signs they have on hotel room doors?"

Dr. Paulson nodded, and Maggie went on. "Well, yeah, but Harriet Linden is going home today and I wanted your opinion on the poem I wrote for her to take with her." She opened her omnipresent pink journal to the right page and held it out for Dr. Paulson. "Well, it's not really a poem in the technical sense, but I think she'll like it anyway."

"Excuse me for a moment," Dr. Paulson said to me as he accepted the journal, "it appears that I've been summoned to a STAT poetry review." He slipped on a pair of reading glasses and read Maggie's work, looked out the window for a moment, then read it once more. Handing the journal back he said, "It's a lovely poem, Maggie, one of your best. But Mrs. Linden has a very difficult prognosis. I'm afraid that a poem like this could be giving her false hope."

Maggie frowned and set the journal on the bed, on top of my medical record. "False hope? You mean, as opposed to true despair? Seriously, Dr. Paulson, how can you give someone false hope? Like the poem says, there's no such thing. It's an oxymoron."

Dr. Paulson stuck his hands deep into the pockets of his long white lab coat. "Maggie, you poets can write about miracles, and God love you for doing it. But we doctors have to face facts and accept reality as it is. And the reality of this situation is that Mrs. Linden probably does not have a whole lot more time."

Maggie looked from the aquarium to the healing tree, then glared defiantly back at Dr. Paulson. "So what if you're right. What if she really doesn't have much time. Does that mean she shouldn't have a hope diamond to wear next to her heart?"

If I hadn't seen for myself Dr. Paulson barking orders in the trauma room – *We're losing her! Get me that trache tube right now!* – I might actually have thought Maggie had intimidated him. "Of course not, Maggie, but as her doctor I really can't encourage her in a state of denial."

Maggie stomped her foot on the floor. Then she reached up and grabbed a handful of flaming red hair and, with a flourish fit for a Hollywood goddess, she pulled it off. Her hair. All of it. She stood there bald as a cue ball glaring at Dr. Paulson. "If it weren't for denial," she snapped, her voice a black panther on a leash, "I'd be dead. Look at me. I have no hair, the figure of a toothpick in tennis shoes, and I throw up every Wednesday at seven after chemo. What kind of guy is going to ask me out for a date? But you know what? My Prince Charming is out there looking for me. And he's going to find me. If that's denial with a capital D, well, I got no problem with that." Maggie stuck the wig back on her head, crooked, and gave it a tug. "Dreams are a whole lot better than reality, whatever the hell that is. Dreams do come true, you know. But sometimes you've got to deny reality to make room for the dream to find a home."

Maggie kept tugging at her wig, trying to get it on reasonably straight, and looked over at me. "Live your dreams before they come true, just in case you never wake up. Now there's a poem for you, Carrie Anne," she said, wagging a finger at me. "McZen wrote it. And it's pretty damned good advice. Remember that." Now she returned her defiant glare to Dr. Paulson.

Dr. Paulson picked up the pink journal from the bed. "Let me read it again." Maggie gave me another surreptitious wink. He cleared his throat, and this time read Maggie's poem out loud, as she watched, arms crossed and foot tapping, like a piano teacher looking over the shoulder of a pupil who had obviously been playing baseball when he should have been practicing his chords.

THE HOPE DIAMOND

The most precious diamond in the world cannot be purchased, it can only be accepted.

The most precious diamond in the world cannot be seen, it can only be felt.

The most precious diamond in the world cannot be worn around your neck, it can only be kept safe in your heart.

The most precious diamond in the world cannot be taken away, it can only be given away.

The most precious diamond in the world is free for the asking, and you can have as many as you ask for.

The most precious diamond in the world is stronger than iron, but more fragile than a dream.

The most precious diamond in the world is always genuine, because there's no such thing as false hope.

He tucked the journal under his arm and said, "let's get a second opinion." Then he turned to me. "What do you think, Carrie Anne? Should a doctor go along with giving a patient hope even when he thinks there is no hope?"

"There's always hope," I said, and even as I was saying it I couldn't believe that I was hearing myself say it.

Dr. Paulson read over the poem once more, silently this time, then handed the pink journal back to Maggie. "It's perfect, Maggie. Harriet will love it. And now, if it's alright with you, I'd like to get back to work here. Okay?"

Maggie gave me one last wink, then skipped toward the door. Before she stepped out of the room, Dr. Paulson called after her. "One more thing, Maggie. After you've printed it up, could you make copies for Carrie Anne and me? And make sure to autograph them. Someday, when you're rich and famous, we'll both be able to say we were there at the first reading."

"Hope flies on silver wings," Maggie chirped as she disappeared through the door. Today she was wearing a t-shirt that said *There's More To Me Than What You See*. I sensed that I was just beginning to glimpse the depth of this young mermaid poet.

MISDIAGNOSIS

Haiku!

Bless You.

Subtle Wisdom –

Is Often Misdiagnosed.

McZen

Chapter Eight

"*B*ye, *Mom. I love you.*" Like the bitter-sweet of salt poured on ice cream, Robbie's parting words touched my soul and broke my heart. He was going to be gone for almost two weeks, on a fishing trip to Canada with his uncle Randy. I wasn't really listening to Maggie as she chattered away, sitting on the windowsill by the healing tree. Rather, I was surrendering to the melancholic inner voice telling me that my son was a three-quarters orphan – no father and only half a mother – and the only remaining proof that I once had been a woman.

"Poem is sort of a weak word, don't you think?" Maggie had a special knack for discerning when I wasn't paying attention to her, and forcing me back with an unanswerable question. I simply shrugged, which seemed to satisfy her that I was sufficiently attuned. "Kind of like dream or love, you know. Or like jazz. The word is so wimpy, you hardly even think of it as being a noun. It doesn't have real substance to it. Like, say, job. Or dollar bill. Words with meat on them. Of course, air doesn't have any real substance to it either, but you can't live without air. Same with love and dreams, and jazz. Can't live without them." Maggie pulled off her wig and tugged at the wild hairs. Then she continued, "For you and me, Carrie Anne, it's the same with poetry. We can't live without it."

"Well, I'm sure that's true for you, Maggie, but I've managed to live without poetry for the past twenty-two years, and I'm sure I'll get by without it for whatever years I have remaining." As she usually did, Maggie had something printed on the front of her T-shirt. I squinted to read it: *I have lots of friends – you just can't see them.* I pointed at her chest. "Your invisible friends – members of the Dead Poets Society?"

"Yeah. Except they're not really dead, you know. As long as someone is reading their poems, a part of them is still alive. That's why you've got to write, Carrie Anne. It's like what Anne Frank said in her diary, that when you write a part of you lives forever."

"Well, writing in her diary sure didn't help Anne Frank live forever."

"Did you ever read her diary?"

"Back in high school."

"So you see – through her diary she was still alive even then, alive enough to talk to you. The only question is, were you listening?"

I closed my eyes and thought back to that high school English class assignment. I couldn't remember a single thing that Anne Frank had written in her diary, but I had a vivid recollection of the emotions I felt while reading about this young girl who could write of love and hope even when she was trapped in a tiny and fragile refuge surrounded by hate and despair. She had been no older than my Robbie. It was more than half a century too late, but I still wanted to reach out and hug that frail child, to protect her from those evil thugs in the brown shirts with the red swastika arm bands who had dragged her away to die, leaving behind only the diary in which her words would live forever. "I was listening, Maggie, only it's taken a long time for me to really hear."

As I lay in bed that night I stared at the healing tree silhouetted by light escaping from the parking lot four floors below. After a while, I flicked on the over-bed lamp, turned on my laptop computer and searched for poems about trees – some I remembered from childhood and some I'd never before seen. Poems by Joyce Kilmer, Lucy Larcom, Robert Frost, Mary Oliver,

William Blake, Gary Snyder, Robert Louis Stevenson, others long forgotten. When I awoke in the middle of the night the light was still on. And this is what I saw in the flickering screen of my laptop.

∧ ∧

∧ ∧ ∧

∧ ∧

                              tre
                           esoflife
                        nothingsolovely
                      asatreebutonlygod
             canmakeatreeblowin dreamedoftreesthat sowasdeath
               inthewindleaves likesailsonlodgepolepines—
                 mastswithoutashiponlygodcanmakeatreemakeatreeonly
            godcanmakcatreebuthegoestosomesuperiortreewithoutaleafandonly
          onlyonlygododcanmakcatrcewhile Iplayedinmytreehousegodwatchedthefallingneedles
       ofthechristmastreeochristmastreelighttakesthetreebutwhocantellushow?anyfoolcan
            writepoetrybutonlygodcanmakeatreemakeatreelikeamightyoakthehealingtreeamig
        htyoakisourlordthatspreadsherrootsdeep anddrinksdeepoftheearthandonlygodcanmakea
     treeanddeadleavesarehardesttobearliftmelikealeafintothewindneverseeapoemaslovelyasatreeonly
      lodgepolepinessoughingonmountaintopswillowsweepingformeastheycaressadyingearth
     ajeweledtreewithglassleavesaglitterinthegoldairagreatmaternalpinewhosebranchesexplaineverythingonly
      theueesdeepeigieeiiyelloweiiiandiedderloudinthepinesandthecedarsdimcoveringearthandfillingheaven
    thebarkofthetreesroughandsexual treesyouplantedaschildren devouredby caterpillarstinyandgreen and monstrousandyellow
      windiswithouthowlsinthetrees fadedfutureuncertainandfrail homeforwhitedovesblowinginthewind
       whentheoldchinesepoetisawakenedunderthefallentreedebatingwhattodowithanaxe,cherryblossomsweeping
        comedancewithmeinthedarkforestandbemyloveunderthehealingtreeandlistentoechoesinthedeepwood
       whatforestsandfruitsarethese?whereEvepickedfruitfromthetreethatmenmightknowoftruthandwonderandsitunder
      thebranchesofthehealingtreewiththephantomoftheforestandthespiritofthetreeinthesacredshadeofthehealingtree
       cuzonlygodcanmakeatreelikethehealingtreeahomeforthebirdsandthebugsandthesquirrelsthehealingtreefalling
        leavesinthewindrootsreachdowntothecavernsofhellandtheentireforestquakesinfearofitsfireswhencomesthem
       anwiththeaxeyoucanhearthefuryofthewindthroughtheleavesbecauseanyfoolcanwieldanaxebutonlygodcanma
        keatreewheretherootsgodownsodeeptoodeepfortearsandthere'snothingkeepsitsyouthbutatreeandtruthandonly
     myfocoutstretchdbeneaththetreepinetreetopsbendsnow bluewhyhaveyouahomeforthewildthingsliketruthandspr
     ingthatonlygodcanmake hewhoplantsatreeplantsahope plantsajoyplantspeaceplantsyouthplantslove treesaretruthonlygod
     anyfoolbutonlygodmygodwhyhaveyou   forsakenmytreeanyfool
       planthopejoypeaceyouthlovetruth   plantatreeonlygodonlygodonlyonlyonly   treesbecamethycross
        andonlygodcanmakeatree   sosimplereallyonlygodonlygodgod   godcanmakeaterrible
      intheforestintheforestwild   ifoundalovelychildfullofwisdomfull   ofgraceandwilddeath
          sycamorestands   whatdoesheplantwhoplantsatreeahomeforbugsandbirdsandbees
                      amightyoak   upon   whichcoolshadeandtenderrain
                 thegloryofthegoldenplain   only   godcanmakeatreeahealingtree
                 thatmakesacrossuponwhich   whyhaveyouforsakenmeochrist
                 mastreeohealingtreeonlygodcan   make   atreemightyoakspreadsherroots
                 deepanddrinksdeepoftheearth   anyfoolbutonlygodmygodwhyhaveyoufor
                 itisfortheloveoftreesthatiwritemy   poetryunderneaththehealingtreeyesany
                     foolcanbutonlygodcanmake thelushdarkcanopiesofthegnarledtrees
                      phantomoftheforest   fromeachbraveeyeshallsproutatree
                        thespiritofthetree   autumnleavesfallingfailing
                        wherethespider   andthewillowweeps
                        ofdeathluresthe   weepsforme
                        flyoflifeintoher
                        webintheleave
                        sofamightyoak   only
                        thatonlygodcan   man
        a   maketreesareho   cancut
       rose   peandloveandfa   down
      isarose   iththatonlyafool   a
     thatrosetobe   wouldforsakean   tree
       atreeandwhatarethosefuzzlylookingthingsoutthere—trees?amillionchristmastreeswaitingfor
      christmasdignifiedtallfirsonlygodtreesarefavoredbythefoggrowfloweringjudasastheoldtreegoeson
      onlygodcanmakeatreegrowinbrooklynwhereisanyeyethatdeservestolookattreesnothingislovelyasatree

Chapter Nine

Maggie and I were sitting in the patient sunroom in our wheelchairs. Her cancer had flared up again and they'd admitted her. With her fuzzy head and her toothpick figure, draped as she was in a hospital gown that would have accommodated three more of her, she looked like a little ragamuffin doll. When I told her that, she opened her pink journal. "Note to self," she said aloud as she wrote in the journal, "write a poem about Maggie the Magamuffin." Most anyone at Memorial Hospital would have caught the double meaning in that poem, because many a morning you could catch the scent of Maggie's special muffin recipe (called, of course, Magamuffins) wafting through patient care unit corridors. Poems for the soul, muffins for the body, as Maggie would say.

Maggie finished writing the note in her pink journal and closed it. "When I first got diagnosed, I was pretty bummed," she said. "I wasn't what you would call a model of positive thinking." Maggie cackled like a six-year-old laughing at the punch line of her own joke. "I started writing poems for the same reason that Saint Exupéry flew airplanes – you know, the guy who wrote *The Little Prince*? To free my mind from the tyranny of petty thoughts. I think it saved my life, back in those desperate lonely times, creating an imaginary sex life filled with romantic couplets and one-night stanzas." Another cackle. "So I thought if writing poems could be part of my healing, then maybe writing them for other people could be part of their healing. And you know what?"

"What?"

"Turns out that sharing poems has been even more important for my own healing than writing them has. Every time I write a poem for someone else, I'll bet I kill a million cancer cells."

"So how did you get a job as the hospital poetry therapist?"

Maggie shrugged. "Just asked for it. I went to see the director of the volunteer department with the idea, and she said yes. I suppose it helped that my application was in the form of a poem."

Maggie pulled her knees up to her chest and rested her chin on them. Without thinking, I tried to do the same, but of course the message got lost somewhere between my brain and my waist. "You'd be surprised," Maggie said, "just how important a simple little poem can be in someone's healing."

"Yeah, I probably would be," I replied. "Before I met you, I'd never even heard of a poetry therapist. In fact, I probably would have laughed at the idea." If Maggie was offended by this comment, she didn't show it.

"I'll tell you about one," Maggie said as she wiggled around in her wheelchair. "Several years ago, I wrote a poem for a mom who'd lost her baby. I said that a baby is like a mermaid on a moonbeam, breathing there inside you. It's magic, and no matter what happens, some bit of that magic, the magic of the mermaid on the moonbeam, is always there." Not for the last time, I marveled at how someone so young could have become so wise. Maggie continued: "A while later, I got a letter from that woman. She told me that of all the piles of paper she'd taken home from the hospital, my poem was the only thing she'd kept, that it was framed on the wall in her bedroom. She didn't keep the clinical notes or the discharge summary or a copy of the hospital bill. Only my poem. So you see, even long after the doctors and nurses had finished their work, and the insurance company paid the bills, my poem is still helping that mom to heal."

My memory went back to the miscarriage I'd had before Robbie was born. I'd left the hospital more than merely grief-stricken; I'd felt that my baby's death had somehow been my fault. How different might my emotions have been had Maggie been there to write me a poem?

"Want to know a secret?" Maggie asked. I nodded. "When the nurses take care of you, it's not just them taking care of you – you're also taking care of them. It's a two-way relationship, whether the two of you know it or not."

"How can I be taking care of my nurses when I'm flat on my back in bed?"

"That doesn't matter. In fact, it might even help you empathize. You've seen how hard the nurses here work, and how stressful their jobs can be. They've got problems at work, they've got problems at home, and they've got to leave all those problems out in the hallway every time they walk into a patient's room. And you know what? Some patients make their nurses sick, and I mean that literally. They don't want to be in the hospital, and they go out of their way to let everyone know it."

"So what can you do?" Even as I asked the question, I knew what the answer was going to be.

"Well, for one thing, you could write your nurse a poem. One of my nurses was going through a really tough time. You'd never have known it just watching her as she worked, but one of her kids had been busted for drugs and she was going through a nasty divorce. I wrote a poem for her, a poem about finding strength in adversity – how it's like stumbling across an oasis in the desert. She cried when I gave it to her. Like maybe this was the first time anyone had recognized that this caregiver also needed to be given some care. It was like my poem was the hug she needed, you know, a hug printed on paper."

"That's a beautiful image, Maggie – a hug on paper. I imagine she has your poem framed up on her wall, too."

Maggie nodded. "Maybe so." We both looked out the window for a while, comfortable with the silence. At last Maggie said, "You should do this, Carrie Anne. You'd make a great poetry therapist."

I just laughed. "Oh, Maggie, you've got to be kidding! Why, I haven't written a poem since the ninth grade. I wouldn't even know where to start."

"It's actually pretty easy," she replied. "You just put yourself in the shoes of the person you're writing for, then write a poem for yourself, the 'you' who's in those shoes. It will come out perfect, every time. Guaranteed."

I laughed again and shook my head. "I'm afraid I'm not creative like you are, Maggie. I don't have a Poetry Muse. And it's not likely that I'll ever step into shoes again, mine or anyone else's."

"Of course you have a Poetry Muse. Everyone has a Poetry Muse. You just need to wake her up. And it's actually good thing you haven't written a poem since ninth grade. That means you have bunches of them stored in your memory banks."

"I doubt it, Maggie. When it comes to poetry, I'm afraid my memory banks are empty because I haven't been making any deposits."

"Then you're going to have to steal some. There's really only one master poem, you know. Everything else is just a variation. Like jazz – poetry is improvisation on that one universal theme. So if you don't have a good idea yourself, just go out and steal one and then jazz with it."

"Steal one! You're kidding, right?"

Maggie cackled and her mint green eyes sparkled, standing out against her fiery crown of fake red hair, reminding me that Maggie was the closest thing to a human Fourth of July fireworks displays that I'd ever known. "No I'm not kidding," she said. "And actually, I even stole that advice – from T. S. Eliot. He said that good poets *borrow*, but great poets *steal*. And he should know, because he was a great poet. And he did both."

"You're very persuasive, young lady," I said, "but I'm afraid I'm too old to start writing poetry now, even if I were to steal ideas."

"Too old?" Maggie cocked her head to the side and frowned. "How old do you have to be to be too old to write a poem?"

Before I could answer, Maggie's nurse walked into the sunroom. She apologized for interrupting, but Maggie was scheduled for a procedure. After they'd left, I started doodling on the notepad I kept in the pouch on the side of my wheelchair. Though I didn't want to admit it, Maggie was right. My memory banks *were* filled to overflowing with poems waiting to be born. I could almost picture them as real physical things. After a very long time of sitting and waiting for my Poetry Muse to show up, I picked up the pen and started to write:

THE ENVELOPE, PLEASE

My memory is an envelope

into which I place my thoughts

and emotions and experiences.

All those poems waiting to be written.

I address it to a Me I don't yet know.

Seal it with a first class kiss.

Drop it into the Big Blue Box.

And pray

that it doesn't get lost in the clouds.

It was the first real poem I'd written since the ninth grade. I have no idea how many hours I spent writing, scratching out, and writing again, so totally did I give myself over to this maiden voyage back into the world of poetry. Maggie, Maggie. The mermaid poet dispensing miracle poems, who herself was so desperately in need of a miracle. As it turned out, being a mermaid was no protection against being eaten by sharks.

MERMAIDS ON MOONBEAMS

I have heard the mermaids singing
Siren songs stretching like aural opium
From the depths of ancient seas
I tie myself to the mast
Resist the tidal pull of those narcotic voices

I long to lie with them in meadows of poppy
To float with them on silver-needled moonbeams
To lie at their feet, bleached bones in the sun
But they leave me singing to myself
A forlorn love song that echoes sadly
Through the hollow chambers of the sea

Maggie Mermaid,
with apologies to Homer and Eliot

Chapter Ten

"So, what did you do before the accident?" I was back in the hospital recovering from the latest operation. Another set of rods and pins pounded and screwed into my body; I am a laboratory for surgeons who work with violent tools.

It's funny how in the hospital, people get to know you from the inside out. Nurse Higgins (her nametag says Suzanne, but everyone on the ward called her Nurse Higgins) knew my potassium levels and the color of the butterfly tattooed on my left boob, but none of the things that any guy would have known five minutes into a blind date. Like what I did before the accident.

"Mark was a branch manager for Wells Fargo," I answered. "I sold real estate part time." Looking over at the wheelchair parked by the window, I again appreciated just what a Great Divide that accident would be in my life. Even the icebreaker questions would change. Instead of "What do you do?" it would forevermore be "What did you do before you were crippled?"

"Think you'll go back to real estate?" Nurse Higgins had finished checking all the lines and tubes and was entering something into a keyboard. She'd probably started her nursing career when I was in diapers, but still had to keep up with the computer revolution.

I shook my head no. "Can you see me driving people around to look at houses in my handicapped van?" I put on my best *you're going to love this cozy little fixer-upper* voice and said, "You two go on in and look around – I'll just park my wheelchair out here at the front steps and wait for you."

Nurse Higgins smiled. "I guess I should have thought of that. Most homes have lots of stairs, don't they?" I shrugged and made a face. She said, "I guess that also means becoming a flight attendant is out of the question, doesn't it?"

"Probably," I replied, "but I might be able to get a job as a redcap. *Just put your bags here on my lap and give me a push.*"

She laughed, then asked, "Did you have any hobbies?"

"Yeah. I was a water aerobics instructor." The ridiculous image of me bobbling around the pool in a wheelchair with water wings instead of wheels caused me to almost laugh. I closed my eyes for a moment to focus on that mental image of me in my water wheelchair, to see where it would take me. A fine mist began to build over my imagined swimming pool. Almost instantly, the mist turned dense, then corporeal. It was snowing. The water in the pool froze solid. I was trapped in the blue ice of a swimming pool that had transmogrified into a glacier. I was the ice baby, sky blue. I shivered and opened my eyes. "I also taught beginner ice-skating lessons, but I don't think that's in my future either. Not unless they come up with a new sport – wheelchair ice-skating."

Nurse Higgins took the stethoscope from around her neck and dropped it into the wide pocket of her white dress. I knew she'd been on her feet all day, but if she ever complained, I never heard it (though I myself would have given every worldly possession to be able to complain about aching feet). "Wheelchair ice skating? That sounds like fun. Except it might turn into wheelchair bumper cars on ice!" Bless her heart, Nurse Higgins had a knack for saying just the right thing to stop me from spiraling back into the frigid gloom. Icebreakers of a different sort.

She looked back at the computer screen and tapped on the keyboard, then looked back at me. "I see you're going to start working with the people from OT. They might even be able to design an ice-skating chair for you. Some of what they do is just plain magic."

I shrugged and shook my head. "OT? Overtime?"

She laughed. "Sorry, I sometimes forget that we hospital people have our own language. OT is Occupational Therapy. They're going to help you learn new ways to deal with ADL. That's hospital-speak for activities of daily living. Their work can end there, or they can push you harder, help you carve out a more productive path for yourself. It's really up to you."

"What do you mean, it's up to me?"

The way she folded her arms, Nurse Higgins reminded me of an old-world schoolmarm trying to get through to a particularly slow student. "I went to nursing school because I wanted to be a caregiver. But unless my patients take an active role, I end up being just a caretaker. You've reached the point where you have to decide – do you want to be an active participant in your recovery, even if it can't be a full recovery, or do you just want to be a passive recipient of my care?" Now the schoolmarm was lecturing the naughty girl who'd been caught skipping class. Not knowing what else to do, I started to cry.

Nurse Higgins sat on the edge of the bed and brushed the hair off my forehead. "I know this is hard, Carrie Anne. And it's always going to be hard. Things that you once took for granted, like going to the ladies room or reaching for a box of cereal on the top shelf, are going to take a lot more time and energy than they did before the accident. And that's going to mean less time and energy for the things that really matter." I pictured myself sitting in my wheelchair at the bagel shop, unseen by the girl behind the tall counter; the Great Divide loomed larger, casting its dark shadow across every facet of the rest of my life. An ice age without end.

Before she left, Nurse Higgins told me a bit more about what I could expect from the folks in Occupational Therapy. She made it clear that the sooner I learned how to cope with the ladies room and the bagel shop, the more time I would have for making a new life – a life without legs. "Who knows," she'd said, "you could even wind up writing poetry like Maggie does. That's how she got started, after all."

The suspicion that Nurse Higgins and Maggie were somehow in cahoots was confirmed shortly when Maggie, the mermaid poet, waltzed into my room about an hour later. She'd been released from the hospital and was back to her usual bubbly self. Today's t-shirt read: *Poetry – Jazz with Words.* I wondered if she meant for "Jazz" to be a verb or a noun, then realized that the one usually leads to the other.

"Whatchya got there?" Maggie asked, craning her neck in the attempt to read the words I'd been scribbling on a notepad.

"It's a lousy poem, if you must know, Miss Mermaid." The frizzy red strands of the latest addition to her wig collection brushed my cheek and I wondered if the woman who'd donated the hair for that wig was on fire the way Maggie was.

"They're all lousy at first," Maggie said as she lifted the pad from my lap before I could yank it away, "but they do get better if you keep working on them." She giggled. "At least some of them do." She read over my poem, nodded thoughtfully, then read it again, her lips moving in sync with my written words:

BLUE ICE

The snow fell and fell – year upon year

Melting, refreezing, condensing – year upon year

Relentlessly layering – year upon year

Crushing the ground beneath – year upon year upon year

Ice harder than Granite

Ice colder than Mars

Ice ancient as Hades

Glacier ice freezing my heart

Trapping every wave of light

Except the blues

The cyanotic sapphire blues

Frozen blue tears come crashing down and

Drift away doomed

To melt in some distant sea

"Keep writing," Maggie said. "For mermaids like you and me, writing poems is the only way to crack the ice. Keep writing, Carrie Anne." She tore off the page with my poem, folded it in half, and stuck it into the pages of her pink journal. "I'll bring this back after I make a copy," she said.

"What do you need a copy for?"

Maggie ignored my question and instead exclaimed, "Man, I got busted today!"

"Busted? What happened? Is everything okay?"

"Oh, yeah, it's really no big deal. I just got thrown out of Taco Bell." She pulled off her wig and held it at her waist, the way a man might hold his cap when he's just learned that he's been laid off from his job.

"Thrown out of Taco Bell! What happened? What did you do?"

"Well, they had a sign out front that said 'Days – $7.50.' That sounded like a pretty good deal to me, so I went in and tried to buy 365 of them. I even wrote out a check for two-thousand, seven-hundred and thirty-seven dollars and fifty cents. That's 365 times seven-fifty. Made it out to Taco Bell and everything." Maggie twisted the wig in her hands, then made a sad face as she rubbed her bald head. "I told the manager I didn't have very many days of my own left, so I wanted to buy a year's worth of his. He threw me out! Can you believe it? I thought he was going to call the cops." Maggie perched the wig on top of her head again, not quite getting it straight. "Man, some people just really need to lighten up, huh?" She gave the wig another tug.

"Maybe you should write him a poem."

"I already did," she replied. "Something about a waitress in a Mexican restaurant dumping a bowl of hot sauce in the lap of a really obnoxious customer. But I don't think I'll give it to him. He'd call the cops for sure!"

Maggie skipped out of my room swinging her pathetic excuse for hips and belting out her own off-key rendition of La Cucaracha. I doodled a little mermaid on the empty page of my notepad, then scribbled out a poem.

BUSTED!

Just when she was starting

to get

the hang

of it,

they revoked her poetic license.

That, they scolded, would teach her

not to go…

so fast.

I read over the new poem again and realized that another blue teardrop had just floated out to sea.

DEAR GOD PLEASE...

make my world stop for a day make my problems go away pay
my bills make up my will clean the house mow the yard fix
the car get my son into braces help dad tie his shoelaces send
letters to my friends let them know that the end is on the way
so they should send those cards and letters now while I still
have time to read them I'll make a cup of tea and sit by the fire
and read their good-byes and while you do the chores I'll write
my replies and we'll just let the machine answer the phone
and when you're all done with the chores dear God I'd like a
minute alone to ask you a question or two

C.A.M.

Chapter Eleven

You know how they say marathon runners hit a wall? Well, I sure as hell was never going to run a marathon, but I had run into a wall. It was almost seven months after the accident (my entire life will always be divided into before and after the accident), and I was back in the hospital. More surgery. More physical therapy. More mind-numbing boredom sitting in that bed waiting for Robbie or Maggie to visit and instead having the shrink or some well-intentioned social worker show up to ask me how I really felt about all of this. For lack of anything better to do, I'd been working on a poem about how to hate a dead man, but I couldn't get past the realization that there's nothing a living person can do to harm someone who is already burning in hell. That was my frame of mind when Maggie came into the room pushing an empty wheelchair.

"It's a gorgeous day outside – a day made for lady poets. Let's go for a ride out to the healing garden. Everything's peaking, Carrie Anne, it's a revolution of color and fragrance. You gotta see it." Maggie loved revolutions. One of the day shift nurses was standing outside the door, and came in to help Maggie transfer me from the bed to the wheelchair.

"If this is part of your endless one woman campaign to turn me into a poetry therapist, young lady, I just want you to know right now that you're wasting your time. So don't get your hopes up."

"Hope is the North Star, Carrie Anne, it comes up by itself." Today she was wearing one of those Prairie Home Companion t-shirts that read:

Party

Of

English

Majors

"I didn't know you were an English major, Maggie." I tried to act nonchalant as Maggie and the nurse whose name I didn't catch used the sheet to life me out of the bed, but still I held my breath, terrified that they might drop me.

"Oh, I'm not an English major," she replied, "I just love poems – and parties."

The hallways were especially crowded today. I'd overheard some of the nurses talking about a flu epidemic. I was still getting used to looking at people at belt buckle level instead of eye level, and to the fact that they almost never looked down at me but instead looked the other way, as if something really fascinating was happening wherever it was that I wasn't.

Once we passed through the doors into the healing garden, I had to keep my eyes closed against the light for the first several minutes, but this only served to heighten the impression of my other senses that somehow a Caribbean breeze had lost its way and ended up at Memorial Hospital. Maggie parked the wheelchair by a bench and sat down next to me. Well, Maggie never really just sat anywhere; she sort of vibrated in one spot for a while. I'm sure that on its very best day the Garden of Eden was never this lovely. The healing garden was green as Ireland, all a-riot with flowers that seemed to have been stolen from a July Fourth fireworks display. For one precarious second I was almost happy, almost at peace with the world and with myself. Then it all came back. I was the broken lady who had lost her husband and who could not take care of her son.

I wrapped my arms around my shoulders, wishing it was Mark I was hugging, that it was Robbie, wishing that the broken lady would give me back my legs, give me back my life, and let me walk through this garden in love instead of sitting forlorn in this wheelchair. Maggie sat cross-legged on the bench scribbling in her journal, oblivious to my distress. At last, she closed her book. I could feel her staring at me, but didn't look back.

"Want to know the one word you most need right now?" From the corner of my eye I could see that Maggie was now perched on the edge of the bench, facing me. "The one word you must absolutely accept if you want to move on with your life? It'll be easy, because you already know the word."

"Sure," I sniffed, still keeping my eyes glued to my useless feet, "what's the word?"

"Was." That's all she said.

"Was?" I shot her a quick glance, then looked back down at my feet. "Was? That's it? Was is the one word that will let me move on with my life?"

"Yep. The day you replace 'why me?' with 'was me,' you start to move from self-pity to acceptance. You need to do that, Carrie Anne, so you can stop crying about yesterday and start dreaming about tomorrow."

Any thoughts I might have had about being cried out were drowned in a fresh downpour. I suppose it was inevitable that sooner or later, somebody was going to give me a tough love talk like this, but never in a million years would I have suspected that somebody would be Maggie.

"Isn't it a funny paradox," she continued, "that the quintessential word of the past – was – is the one word that can free you from the past. It *was* you, Carrie Anne, sitting in the passenger seat of that car. It *was* you who survived when Mark didn't. Every time you ask yourself the unanswerable why – why me? – you're poking your hand into the steel trap of the dead past." Maggie leaned closer, so that her nose almost brushed against my cheek. "Do you know what a coyote does when she gets her paw caught in a trap?"

"Chews it off?" I sniffled.

"That's right." Maggie put a hand on my shoulder and whispered, "She knows it's better to be a three-legged coyote than a four-legged fur coat."

I had this sudden mental picture of a three-legged coyote. Something like you'd see in a cartoon – peg-legged Wiley E. Coyote on crutches after having once again been outsmarted by the road runner. You know the kind of mess you can make when you cry and laugh at the same time? God help me, I couldn't help myself. The image of that poor old 3-legged coyote, hobbling around on a crutch, had me doubled over in my wheelchair. I hadn't laughed like this in months, and until now hadn't realized how badly I needed to laugh. Every time Maggie and I looked at each other, it ignited another round.

Heaven knows how many people were chased out of the Healing Garden by our cackling and howling. I'm sure we sounded like a couple of old coyote mommas howling coyote hymns under a full desert moon. I didn't care. Something was happening in that garden, something as ancient as giving birth, something as defining as being a woman. Laughing through our tears, letting go even as we hung on, the three-legged coyote and I celebrated a secret sacrament known by every woman since Eve, each in her own time and in her own way. Embracing the pain, accepting the loss, chewing off a paw and moving on – limping, but free.

Maggie pulled off her wig and threw it at me and, to my surprise, I caught it and threw it right back at her. This ignited another round of raucous laughter as we threw the wig back and forth, each taking dead aim at a spot between the other's eyes and missing by a mile. I wondered if the hospital security guards might come out and arrest us for disturbing the peace of the healing garden. When we finally settled down, Maggie opened up her pink journal. "Want to hear the poem I just finished?"

I wanted to reach over and rub her precious bald head but she was too far away so I just said, "Sure, Maggie, I'd love to hear your new poem."

"It's called The Snake and I. With apologies to Robert Frost."
As she always did before reading one of her poems, Maggie tried
to compose herself and look serious, which only made her more
ludicrous, this pixie stick with a cue ball head inset with flashing
green eyes and adorned with a drunken sailor's smile. She
cleared her throat and straightened her shoulders. Then she read:

> The snake and I
>
> Both have two eyes
>
> A sensitive tongue
>
> But only one lung
>
> We have to slither
>
> Hither and thither
>
> We love hot rocks
>
> Don't like to wear socks
>
> The snake and I
>
> We believe in the sky
>
> We love our brothers
>
> And obey our mothers
>
> We want to do good
>
> But we're misunderstood
>
> We'd rather be eagles
>
> Or cute little beagles
>
> But we accept who we are
>
> And that has made all the difference

"That's the road less traveled, the fork in the road where
we each have to decide, Carrie Anne. 'Was You' happened and
will not unhappen. 'Is You' is what you decide to become on the
other side of this fork in the road." Maggie put an arm across my

shoulder and kissed my cheek. "You're a lot stronger than you think you are, you know."

I wiped my nose on my sleeve, thankful for being in hospital garb. "I know," I replied in a most unconvincing manner.

"And it's going to be easier than you think it will be, especially when you look back on it from the future."

"I know." Even less convincing.

"You can't do any more than all you can do, Carrie Anne. Sometimes all you can do isn't very much. But even then, all you can do is enough. You just need to swim far enough to reach the next island, not across the whole ocean." We both looked out across the healing garden pond, and for the first time I realized that there actually was a little island in the middle. "And you're lucky," Maggie continued. "You've got a mermaid to swim alongside you."

This time I just nodded, and imagined that after she'd chewed off her paw, the three-legged coyote must have spent many days slinking around in misery before she would again revel in her freedom. Maggie scribbled away in her journal for a minute or so, then said, "want to hear the poem I just started?"

"Sure, Maggie, I'd love to hear it." *Anything to get my mind off these useless legs that I can't chew off.*

"Okay. Only I won't be able to finish it."

"No? So who's going to finish it if you don't?" Even as I heard the words coming out of my mouth, I knew I'd just set myself up.

"You are."

"Me? I can't finish your poem, Maggie. I can't even write my own poems. How could you expect me to finish one of yours? I can already hear the derisive laughter."

"They always laugh at poets, Carrie Anne. At least, they laugh until the poets are famous. Then they stroke their chins and say 'my, that's brilliant,' like they always knew you'd be famous." She cackled her trademark cackle and gave her wig a tug, trying to get it straight and actually making it worse. I tried to not laugh, and she tried to not notice me trying to not laugh. "The bad news," she said, "is that poets usually don't get famous until after they've been dead for a while."

"Well, that's reassuring. So what's the title of your new poem?"

"The Meaning of Life."

"The Meaning of Life? You want me to finish your poem about the meaning of life?"

"Yeah. Want to hear what I have so far?"

"Sure, Maggie, read it to me."

"Okay. Here goes." She adjusted herself on the bench, closed her eyes, and took a deep breath. She tried to look serious, but came across more like a preacher who'd showed up at a funeral after having had several drinks too many. "Okay," she intoned, "here goes. The Meaning of Life, by Maggie Mermaid."

> Today is the day
> The mayflies, newborn, must die
> And in the dying light
> Mosquitoes land and bite

Maggie closed her pink journal and looked up expectantly, saying nothing. "That's it?" I asked. "That's your poem about the meaning of life?"

"Well, it's not finished yet, but yeah, that's it. If you can answer those two questions, you'll solve the riddles philosophers have struggled with for more than two thousand years."

I thought about what she'd just read. "Sorry, Maggie, two questions? Were there questions in your poem?"

"Well, yeah! Like, if you knew why God created mosquitoes, then you'd know why evil exists in the world. Mosquitoes are evil creatures with no redeeming value at all. And if you knew why those cute little mayflies have to die on the same day they're born, then you'd know why bad things happen to good people. What else is to know? Not even Socrates could answer those two questions."

"And you want me to – to finish this poem of yours about mayflies and mosquitoes and the meaning of life?"

Maggie laughed and held the pink journal against her chest. "Sure I do, Carrie Anne. It's easier than you think it will be. And you're stronger than you think you are."

Maggie had to leave to read a poem for a new patient, but said she'd come back for me in an hour. I pulled my hospital gown up over my thighs. In ancient cultures the sun was thought to have magical life-giving powers. I contemplated the scarred and shriveled stalks that had once carried me to mountaintops, and prayed that the sun would return life to them. A mosquito landed on a spot just above my knee, sniffed around for a moment, then flew away without taking a bite.

The journey of
a thousand miles
begins with a
longing inward glance

Far off in the distance
I see the person I am meant to be
It will be a long journey
I must walk slowly

McZen

Chapter Twelve

I felt like I was driving the wrong way down a one-way street. Everything was backwards. Robbie was my chauffeur, and I was going to visit Maggie, instead of Maggie chauffeuring Robbie to come visit me. She was in the outpatient cancer center for another round of chemo. Robbie had picked me up in my hospital room and was pushing my wheelchair through the hospital corridors. On our way, we stopped at the gift shop to buy Maggie a pack of wintergreen Lifesavers, which was just about the only thing she could hold down when she was going through chemo.

I waited out in the corridor watching people go by as Robbie went in. I could see from the entrance that maneuvering a wheelchair through the gift shop would be beyond his navigational aptitude. People walked by, pretending to not see me parked there by the door. Once more, I had a glimpse of the future I'd been trying so hard to not see. Since the accident, I'd been living in a cocoon, moving back and forth between the hospital and the rehab unit. Everything was taken care of for me. I got fed (or at least they brought food and encouraged me to eat it). I had help getting to and from the bathroom. Someone always came when I woke up in a panic in the middle of the night and hit the nurse call button. Someone always cleaned up after me when I made a mess.

In rehab the other day, Amanda the physical therapist had said something about cars with special controls for paraplegics, but I'd parked that tidbit in the same mental compartment where I keep the Rings of Saturn and the Great Wall of China. Sitting there alone in the corridor, though, I understood in a very real way that when she'd said life would be different, she meant that *everything* would be different. Shopping at the mall, paying for an ice cream cone at Baskin Robbins, getting onto an airplane, everything. I knew I couldn't do it without Mark, also knew I wouldn't have that choice.

"Okay, Mom, ready to roll?" Robbie laid a bag that obviously contained more than a pack of Lifesavers on my lap, patted my shoulder, and started us moving down the corridor again.

"Mind if I look?" I asked as I opened the sack and peered inside. "What's this?" I reached in and pulled out one of those little stuffed animals that are a staple of hospital gift shops everywhere. Only it wasn't an animal. It was a mermaid. "Oh, Robbie. This is perfect! She'll love it!"

"I couldn't resist," Robbie replied. "You know Maggie and her thing for mermaids." For just a second, the wannabe grandmother in me imagined Robbie and Maggie – the two most important people in my life – finding each other the way Mark and I had found each other. *Let's see: Robbie's almost 16, Maggie's 26. Hmmm. Might have to wait on that one.* At the bottom of the sack I noticed a folded piece of paper and started to pull it out.

"No. Not that," Robbie said as he reached over my shoulder and yanked the bag out of my hands.

"Why, young Mr. Murphy, was that a little love note I was about to read?" I would have given anything to see the look on Robbie's face, but couldn't get my neck to twist around that far.

"Ah, Mom, you know Maggie's just a friend. And anyway, she's too old for me, and she's still not my type. Besides, I don't have time for girls. At least not till I'm done with medical school."

"Medical school? You're getting pretty serious about that, aren't you?"

"Yeah. Dr. Paulson's been telling me about being a doctor, and I really think that's what I want to do. I know it's hard to get into medical school and all, but I think I can do it."

"I know you can do it, Robbie." I smiled on the outside and cried on the inside. I was going to lose my little boy to medical school. "You've got too much of your father in you to let anyone tell you otherwise. But..." I bit my tongue. How could I tell Robbie, who really was his father's son, that he could do anything he wanted to do – so long as he did it within driving distance of his crippled mom?

"But what?"

Instead of saying what was really on my mind – *you can do anything, Robbie, anything at all, except leave your poor mother alone in that house all by herself* – I said, "But if the right girl comes along, just remember that someday I would like to be a grandmother, okay?"

"Cheez, Mom, I'm not even 16. I'm afraid you're going to have to be patient about being a Grandma." I nodded my acquiescence, but thought to myself how much harder it is to be patient when you've seen the hourglass.

As Robbie pushed me down the long corridor toward the outpatient cancer center, it struck me that everyone was either impatiently waiting for something or rushing to get somewhere else. Nobody seemed particularly content to just be where they were.

When we reached the cancer center, Robbie walked right up to the counter and asked for Maggie. Cheerful and self-assured. *Just like Mark.* We were directed to treatment room 8. Maggie was sitting in one of those big leather chairs with the IV pole towering above her, eyes shut and pink journal sitting closed on her lap. Robbie parked me and gently tapped her on the shoulder. "Hey, Maggie, how's it going?" She opened her eyes and smiled that big smile of hers and said it was going fine, but it was quite obviously not going fine. She was pale and gaunt, and could easily have hidden behind the IV pole. I tried to hide my shock at how frail she looked, and we both laughed at trying to hug each other without falling out of our respective thrones. Then Robbie gave her the bag with the Lifesavers and the mermaid, which she of course said was the most precious thing she'd ever seen.

Maggie and I made small talk while Robbie zoned out with one of the magazines piled up on the little table by the window. When we ran out of things to say, we just sat in silence for a while. She drummed her fingers a-tap a-tap across the cover of the pink journal a few times then said, "You know they're opening that new wing in April? The Women's Center?"

I'd heard something about a construction project of some sort, but mostly from overhearing people complain about how hard it was to find a parking space. "So they're building a center for just us girls? That'll be nice."

"Yeah," Maggie replied, "and it's going to mean more patients. And that means more poems." She nodded solemnly. "Lots more poems."

"Maggie, Maggie, never say die. But you are *not* going to talk me into writing poems with you. I don't write poetry. I *can't* write poetry."

"Did I hear you utter that forbidden word? Can't?" Maggie wagged a scolding finger at me.

"Yeah, Mom, you're not supposed to say you can't do something." Robbie suspended his zombie impersonation long enough to inject himself into the debate. "You can do anything if you put your mind to it. At least, that's what you and Dad always told me."

"Alright," I replied, "how's this: I really don't have time to write poetry. Give me another hundred years or so, though, and I might give it a try." I crossed my arms to let them know that this conversation was over. But out of the corner of my eye I saw Robbie wink at Maggie.

Maggie reached into the gift shop bag and pulled out the folded page that Robbie hadn't wanted me to see. The two of them exchanged an in-the-know glance. Unfolding it, she read it to herself with evident satisfaction, then smoothed it out across the cover of her pink journal. "Alright, Carrie Anne, just one question before we let it go." She looked at me, then at Robbie, who was sitting there looking like the coyote that ate the canary. "I'm going to read you a poem, and you guess who wrote it." Now she winked at Robbie, and he nodded in return. "Okay?" Maggie didn't wait for my agreement, which I'm not sure I'd have given anyway. She just started to read:

GOOD QUESTION – A POEM

What was before
>the beginning of time?
What happens after
>she writes her last rhyme?

What lies beyond
>the outside of space?
What's on the inside of
>his innermost trace?

Who was the architect?
>Who wound the clock?
What keeps it all going
>when you'd think it should stop?

Is the infinite universe
>more than it seems?
Awake I ask questions
>that are answered in dreams.

When she'd finished, Maggie folded the page in half and slid it into the covers of her pink journal. "Who wrote that poem, Carrie Anne?"

I didn't need to answer. All three of us knew. Maggie had just read the poem I'd written for Mr. Brightwood's ninth grade English class. The first real poem I'd ever written. Until quite recently, the last real poem I'd ever written. And then, the strangest thing happened. Instead of remembering that awful silence in the classroom after my words had sunk beneath the linoleum floor, I recalled the way I'd felt when I was actually working on the poem. Nothing else mattered. I couldn't have told you how many hours had flown by, what I'd missed on television, what the other kids were doing outside. It was just me and the words of my poem.

Maggie smiled and nodded and didn't need to say what she was about to say because I could see the words in her eyes. *See, Carrie Anne. All these years you've forgotten the things that matter because you've been remembering things that don't matter. You don't write poetry to impress other people, you write poetry because it's in your heart and it needs to come out.*

I glared at Robbie, not doing a very good job of feigning anger. "So, you've become part of Maggie's little conspiracy, have you? And just where did you find that, young man?"

"When Uncle Randy and I were getting the house ready for a wheelchair, I found it in a box in the back of your closet. Geez, Mom, it wasn't even framed! So I made some copies and had the original matted and framed. Now it's up on the wall at home."

"Made some copies? For who, other than Maggie?"

"Oh, you know, just all of our friends and relatives... And the newspaper."

"You didn't!"

Robbie didn't answer. Both he and Maggie were laughing too hard to talk. And as I laughed along with them, I had this mental image of Mr. Brightwood's linoleum floor cracking open the way the ground cracks open when a sunflower seedling is pushing its way up toward the sun.

THE PEN...

Must truly be mightier than the sword
Else why would I be so afraid
of that pen
Lying unsheathed
On my writing table?

C.A.M.

Chapter Thirteen

After Maggie's chemotherapy was finished, someone from the cancer center took me back to my room so Robbie could wheel Maggie down to the cafeteria; banana milkshakes had been added to wintergreen Lifesavers on the list of things she could hold down after her treatments. I asked to be parked in front of the window by the healing tree, where I could enjoy the warmth of the summer sun and the birds singing in her branches (at least they were there in my imagination). *What was before the beginning of time?* God only knows. Before she wrote her last rhyme, I had choices to make. But first, there was a demon to defeat.

In my ninth grade English class, we'd been assigned to write a villanelle. I couldn't do it. It was too overwhelming, trying to write a poem in which specific lines and rhymes had to be repeated in a prescribed structure. The thought of getting an F for not doing the assignment was far less terrifying than the prospect of humiliating myself by reading childish claptrap in front of the class. The day before it was due, I'd gone to Mr. Brightwood in tears, apologizing and asking to be excused from the homework. He'd told me not to worry, that I could still find a job as a clerk or a waitress without knowing anything about poetry.

Sitting in the warmth of the afternoon sun, I closed my eyes and watched old memories float through my head as they randomly popped up to demand my attention. I saw myself at the state swim meet, where I'd placed second in the distance freestyle event, and even now wasn't sure why I was crying when I received my medal. I saw myself on the lifeguard stand at the city swimming pool when Mark Murphy, one of the popular boys at school, did a cannonball right in front of me, provoking my wrath to get my attention. I recalled those two awful years when Mark was away at business school while I finished up my degree. The day he came home to stay. The day he proposed.

Then, a memory long frozen in the farthest reaches of mental Siberia crept out, an orphan child begging to finally be recognized. It was April of my senior year at the University, and I still didn't have a clue what should come next. So I'd made an appointment with the career counselor. At the end of our session, she'd asked me what I would do if every job paid the same and had the same social status. "I'd be a poet," I'd answered without thinking. She thought I was kidding. So did I.

And now, listening to the invisible birds chirping away in the branches of the healing tree, the question came back to me. Given that being a flight attendant or a water aerobics instructor weren't options anymore, what would I do if the only thing that mattered was doing something I really wanted to do? Something I loved to do. Something I *had* to do.

As a real estate agent, my greatest joy had never been making the sale; it was visiting the new owners a month after the close and seeing how happy they were in their new homes. *What would I do if every job paid the same?* Be a poet? No, there was something missing in that answer. Be a poetry therapist?

Outside my window the sun was putting on a dazzling display for the end of the day. *Red sky at night, mermaid's delight.* In the aquamarine afterglow, I wheeled myself over to the bedside table and pulled out my pad and a pen. I knew I could never be a poet, or a poetry therapist, until I confronted the fears that had blocked me since the ninth grade. Until I put to rest the ghost of Mr. Brightwood. Until I composed my villanelle.

The nurse came by to give me my evening medications. I kept writing. My dinner sat untouched on the overbed table. I kept writing. The nurse's aide came in to check my water pitcher and close the shades. I kept writing. As the drafts progressed from hideous to awful to merely mediocre, I kept writing. What had started as a brand new pad of paper had been whittled down to its last few leaves when I finally stopped. I read over the final draft one more time. *Es freut mich.* One of the few phrases I'd remembered from German class. *It pleases me.* Didn't matter if it didn't please anyone else. Rest in Peace, ghost of Mr. Brightwood. I pulled the last page off the pad and read my villanelle aloud to the empty room.

INVISIBLE TEARS

Dying dreams cry invisible tears.
To mourn the dauntless child that was you
who, now grown, has failed to act in the face of her fears.

You accepted low bid from fate's auctioneer,
only to find his account was past due,
while your dreams in their dying cried invisible tears.

Whatever happened to that brave pioneer,
the girl who dreamed of adventures in your oversized shoes,
in those days before you flinched in the face of your fear?

A once lovely future now stands in arrears –
but it's never too late for old dreams to renew –
when you decide to stop crying those invisible tears.

The terror you feel is just sham veneer,
a Potemkin storefront with a fraudulent view,
meant to keep you from acting in the face of your fear.

When you stand firm, fear (that coward) disappears.
So look in God's mirror, see the meant-to-be you.
Wipe from your cheeks those invisible tears
by choosing to act in the face of your fears.

When the evening nurses came in to move me from the wheelchair to my bed, I was crying. Crying real, visible, human tears. They were the tears of a dream that, having spent too many years sharing a tomb with Lazarus, was now ready for a rebirth of its own.

After the accident, some well-meaning people told me that everything happens for a reason, as if Mark's death and my paralysis were just part of God's master plan. I don't believe that for one second. Such things do not happen for a reason, and certainly not because God has willed them to happen. The meaning and purpose (the reason, if you will) only emerge long after the fact, and then only after you've chosen to follow your dreams, even if it means acting in the face of your fears.

Chapter Fourteen

Maggie was back to her old self. She and I sat by the pond in the healing garden. Maggie was a treasure chest of paradox and contradiction, an insouciant lemon frosting piled deep atop a rich chocolate fudge layer cake. She'd taken off her wig and was sitting cross-legged, eyes closed like a scrawny Buddha statue in the grass, the sun soaking into her bald head like honey dissolving in warm tea. From the middle of the pond, a duck armada approached our little coastline, a fact I was not alone in noticing.

"Hurry, Mommy! Here come the ducks! Let's go!"

Sprinting across the grass charged a little girl who couldn't have been much more than two. Her pink and green floral dress flounced off chubby thighs, and taffy-pull pigtails jutted out at right angles from each side of her head. Her fat little fist clutched a bag of breadcrumbs that was hanging partway open, leaving a Hansel and Gretel trail behind her. She was hurtling forward toward her rendezvous with the ducks at such a furious pace that her little feet could barely keep up. Right in front of us, they failed in their task altogether and she sprawled out face first on all fours.

The little girl picked herself up and with an air of quiet dignity smoothed her dress. She was about to retrieve her bag of bread crumbs when she noticed Maggie. From the look on her face, you'd have thought Maggie had three eyes and a purple nose. The little girl craned her neck toward Maggie with an intensely inquisitive stare. Maggie smiled and wiggled her fingers, which seemed to startle the little girl enormously. Her eyes narrowed into a tight squint and she gawked at Maggie the way one might observe a strange bug under a magnifying glass in science class. Out of the corner of my eye I saw her mother approaching, but the child's gaze never wavered. When her mom arrived, the little girl pointed at Maggie and spoke with solemn urgency.

"Look, Mommy! Missus Potato Head!"

The mother glanced at the two of us without acknowledging our presence, then scooped up the child and hurried on toward the lake. "Come on, Annie," I heard her say. "Let's go feed the ducks." As they walked away, the little girl peered back over her mother's shoulder. Then she smiled a shy smile and wiggled her fingers at Maggie. "Bye-bye Missus Potato Head."

We both laughed until it hurt, until I nearly fell out of my wheelchair. My arms ached to hold that precious little child. I wanted to ask the mother if she was really awake, if she truly appreciated what a gift had been entrusted to her care. I wanted to ask the father if he had any idea what he was missing while he was off making a living so he could make payments on all the things he was giving his family in lieu of himself. "Too bad Mom didn't appreciate the humor in that," I said to Maggie.

"That's because grown-ups are stupid," she replied. Today her t-shirt read *Living is Temporary; Life is Permanent.* "They think things like poverty and cancer are contagious, so poor people and sick people scare them to death. They run away and pretend not to see. God, I'm glad I'll never have to be a grown-up!"

Maggie was like a light switch. She was either on or off, and at any given moment there was no mistaking whether she was walking in her own light or passing through a valley of darkness. And she could, as she just had, go from one state to the other at the flick of an invisible switch.

"What's the matter, Maggie? What stupid thing have we grown-ups done that have you so annoyed today?"

Maggie crossed her arms and glared across the lake. "Marty is dead."

It took a moment for that to register. Marty was one of Maggie's special patients. She'd been writing poems for him since he'd been diagnosed with liver cancer. Even after he went home from the hospital, she kept sending him poems. I felt Maggie's darkness envelop me as well. It had been such a beautiful day, and my brief encounter with that sweet little girl had been so magical, that death's roaring waterfall – almost always in hearing distance of late – had momentarily faded away. Now it was again right around the bend. "Oh, no! When did it happen?"

"Yesterday." Maggie scowled, pulling her arms even tighter into her chest and slouched down on the grass like the rebellious teenager she only recently had grown out of being. "He killed himself. His wife found him in the garage with a hole in his head."

For an instant I thought I might be losing my sanity. I heard banshee voices shrieking in every corner of my mind, felt myself standing directly under that lethal waterfall, icy stinging pellets crashing down on my shoulders, pounding me into inevitable submission. I closed my eyes, and as clearly as though I'd been there myself, the image of Marty crystallized, lying inert on a concrete floor with a midnight-black gun still clutched in his dead hand, blood oozing from his thoughtless brain into a hellish purple puddle on the ground. My scope of vision widened and I could see his wife standing at their garage door, hands over her mouth, too horrified even to scream, her mind forever branded with this hideous image of a murdered husband that would haunt every waking and sleeping hour for the rest of her life.

I took a few slow breaths and prayed for a moment of respite from the banshees. The image slowly dissolved and the voices receded. I opened my eyes. Maggie was tightly clenched into herself, pursed lips barely controlling the angry tirade I knew was going through her head. "Stupid jerk." She spit the words out like a baby ejecting pureed peas.

"You don't know, Maggie." I would have given anything to be able to get out of the wheelchair and sit next to her, to wrap her up in my arms. "None of us know what kind of pain Marty was feeling, or what kind of demons had finally taken over in his mind. Dr. Chandrashar once told me that liver cancer is one of the worst things imaginable."

"Yeah, well I can imagine worse," Maggie retorted. "How about seeing your husband's brains spattered across your garage floor because he didn't have the courage to die the way God meant for him to die? How about being called out of class and told your dear daddy had just put a bullet through his brain without so much as a by-your-leave?"

I didn't know what to say. I watched the little girl in her summer dress and pigtails run chasing after the ducks and wondered what kind of father she had waiting at home for her, or if she even had a father at home, and whether it would really make a difference in how her life eventually turned out.

Maggie was still frozen in her own embrace. I looked out across the pond and prayed for the right words to say, comforting words, but nothing came. What could I possibly say to this young woman who was fighting so desperately to save the remaining fragments of her own life when she saw other people throwing their lives away? Suddenly, though, her internal switch tripped again and her face softened with a smile. "Hey, I've got a new poem," she said. "Want to read it? Maybe you can help me out with it. Something's missing."

"Sure, Maggie, I'd love to read your poem." She handed me her pink journal. It was, I realized, the first time she'd ever done that. Before she'd always read her poems to me. In fact, other than Dr. Paulson that one time, I didn't recall ever having seen her let anyone else ever even touch her precious pink journal. I leaned over to rub her on the shoulder, then I read her poem.

MY PRINCE

Someday my Prince will come,

My Funny Valentine, playing a horn.

Miles he will travel to find me.

A love song, is it? These delicate notes all draped in blue,

That stretch longingly from his golden mouth,

Desperate to find me in my intimate hiding place.

He would slay dragons, this prince of mine.

My Funny Valentine, swinging a sword.

Carry me on his black war horse

To the mountain castle that will be our home.

Father my children, he will –

Boys sturdy and daring.

Girls pretty and wise.

Someday my Prince will come,

My Funny Valentine, bringing me flowers.

He will lay them at my feet

and play for me on his golden horn.

Then he will go away

Alone.

His dying notes will drift forlorn into the evening.

Lonely loving fingers all of blue that will touch me

In my intimate hiding place.

All is well.

Sleep in peace.

God is nigh.

I laid Maggie's pink journal down on my lap. "It's a wonderful poem, Maggie, a beautiful poem. Nothing's missing. Nothing, that is, except a happy ending."

Maggie laughed, but it was just an ordinary laugh, not her usual hysterical cackle. "Well, I tried ending it with Zip-A-Dee Doo-Dah, you know, but somehow Taps seemed to work better. Oh well, thanks for reading it. But listen, I gotta go." Maggie patted me on the knee. "I'm gonna go see Marty's wife. God knows what I'll say to her, but I have a feeling anything I can say will be better than what she's hearing right now."

"I'm sure God does know what you'll say," I replied, "and when the time comes, he'll let you in on it as well." I couldn't decide: at that moment, was I angry at the god I didn't believe in, or did I not believe in the god I was angry at? How could God stand aside and look the other way and let things like this happen? How is it that Maggie, of all people, got delegated to be his emissary to this woman in her moment of grief?

Maggie pulled on her wig. "Is it straight?" I nodded, though in truth you could never really tell when Maggie had her wig on straight. She laughed and started back toward the hospital entrance in her inimitable walk-skip-run. "Write me a poem," she shouted back over her shoulder, "and make it a good one." Then she disappeared into the doors.

Write you a poem? I looked out at the lonely little island in the middle of the pond. One tiny scrubby bush made its home there, like the candle on a one-year-old's birthday cake. *Write you a poem?* About what, Maggie? About running away from life? About someone who's so lonely that instead of boyfriends her poetry is populated with dead jazz musicians? About a young woman who should be writing sonnets of love and instead writes her own death poem? What do you want me to write you a poem about, Maggie?

Down by the water the little girl had stopped chasing the ducks and was sitting quietly by her mother, thumb in her mouth. Where was her Daddy right now? Did he have any clue what he was missing? Could anything he was doing possibly be more important than sitting with this sweet little girl who would not be two for very much longer, and would all too soon be twenty, and maybe dead and buried before seeing twenty-one? Was he, like Marty, sitting in a garage somewhere with a gun in his hand, perhaps ready to run away from life? I picked up my journal and pen. I needed to write a poem for Maggie – a good one. I scribbled:

THE HISTORY OF LIFE

Alone

    Alone Together

      Together Together

        Together Alone

    Alone Alone

Alone

I laughed and closed the journal. "I'm afraid this just won't cut it, Miss Murphy. You're going to have to do better than that!" It was the voice of my ninth grade English teacher. One of the things that made my self-doubt such a formidable foe was its ability to transmogrify into a presumed voice of authority. Even though I knew at an intellectual level the voice was a fraud, it sounded so real and so convincing, once it had spoken the battle was often lost. "Please," I whispered, looking up at whatever lay beyond those fluffy white clouds, "give me a poem for Maggie. And make it a good one." It took a while, but at last I felt ready to pick up my pen and journal again:

FOR MAGGIE

Come running to me in the darkness
        Leave your terror outside my door
Stay with me safe until morning
        By my side till we reach that far shore
In sun and through storm I will hold you
        Through death's door you won't walk alone
Hold my hand as we pass through this valley
        Walk with me, Child, and I'll take you home
Around us we see our friends falling
        Endure pain as our own bodies fail
But as we walk toward the gates to forever
        We know that our souls will prevail
So stay with me now until death do us part
        Leave behind all the fear and the pain
Sing happy songs of the morning
        Till night closes round us again
You're the daughter I always had hoped for
        The granddaughter I might never know
My sister who died as a baby
        The dear friend I'll never let go

I was crying when I closed the journal. In the back of my mind I could hear the voice of the fake ninth grade teacher congratulating me for at least having graduated to tenth grade. I didn't care. I didn't write it for him.

Chapter Fifteen

The healing tree was dying. I was trying to write a letter to Robbie, but all I could think about was dying. Outside, a hard rain beat against the window. Dying weather. The healing tree had been a symbol for what little hope I'd had. If those tiny roots could nourish that baby tree, then perhaps someday my broken roots would sustain me. Now, the healing tree was dying, and it felt like I was too.

I wadded up my latest attempt at a letter and tossed it in the direction of the wastebasket. I wished Maggie would stop by for a visit. She'd been admitted again, but even that didn't stop her from making her poetry rounds. In a few days, I was being transferred from the inpatient unit back to the rehab hospital for what they said would be my final admission before being sent home. I was terrified. I felt like a baby bird about to be pushed out of the nest, even though she had broken wings. I needed a Maggie-gram.

Whenever I got depressed, Maggie would tell me to write a poem about it. It's therapeutic, she would say. *A poem is a dance with your soul, in which you let your soul take the lead.* Maggie was big on soul stuff. I just wondered how you could dance with your soul when your legs didn't work.

What the heck, I finally thought. The letter to Robbie's not materializing. Why not scribble out a poem. I could barely see the parking lot through the rain, and noticed that the healing tree had lost another leaf. Too bad Edgar Allen Poe was dead. Now *he* could have written a poem to capture the spirit of this cold room.

Poe didn't show up, so I was on my own. I scribbled down a few words, scratched them out, then scribbled a few more. *Don't think too much.* I could almost hear Maggie's voice. *Just watch your hand move the pen and let yourself be surprised by what it writes.* Only later, after I'd seen some of the many drafts that Maggie's "simple" poems went through before they were ready for their intended audience of one special patient, did I appreciate how much painstaking work she'd put into watching her own hand move a pen. I scribbled a few more lines, then again scratched them out.

It's okay. Feel what you feel and write about that. Again, Maggie's voice from nowhere. I watched the rain, falling cold and hard on the outside of the window, and the healing tree, dying on the inside. Then I watched my hand start to move the pen across the page:

And the First Shall Become Last

> You never forget the first time –
> That honeydew morning of spring aborning,
> When God takes you by the hand and
> Shows you the splendor of the Garden.
>
> You never expect the last time –
> The basaltine darkness of a dying winter night
> When God, being busy elsewhere,
> Forgets to wake you up.

I read it over once, then the tears started. Tears for Mark, tears for Robbie, tears for Maggie, tears for the broken lady. My life was spiraling downward, out of control, circling the drain. I wanted to die so I could be with my husband, I needed to live so I could be with my son. And God was busy elsewhere.

"That's a beautiful poem." Maggie – the real flesh-and-blood Maggie – stood behind my wheelchair draped in a hospital gown, and was gently rubbing my shoulders as she read the poem sitting in my lap.

"It's not beautiful," I said through my tears. "It's ugly. And I meant it to be ugly."

"It's authentic. And that makes it beautiful. I'm sure that whatever God is doing, even if he's busy elsewhere, he'll hear this. God's always listening, you know, and he knows that sometimes poems are cries for help." Maggie went into the bathroom and came out with a wet face cloth. She wiped away the tear tracks, then put some lotion on my parched lips. "We've got company coming, so we need to make you presentable."

"Company? Who's coming?"

"Jerry Landerall. He's the hospital groundskeeper. He's going to take a look at the healing tree. I'm afraid this little tree can't go to rehab with you next week. She needs some rehab of her own."

There was a knock on the door.

"Come on in, Jerry," Maggie chirped, as though it was her room, and not mine, into which she was inviting this strange man.

Jerry was tall, like Mark, with sandy hair and a bushy mustache. His handshake conveyed the rough gentleness of a man who'd planted many things. We chatted for a moment, then he turned his attention to the healing tree.

"Can you do it?" Maggie looked from the healing tree to Jerry and back again, bouncing on her toes the while. With her hospital gown trailing almost to the ground, she reminded me of one of those happy ghosts that haunt department store candy aisles in the weeks before Halloween.

Jerry stooped to one knee and inspected the healing tree, palpating each leaf, then gently pressed a finger into the soil. At length, he rose and stuffed his hands into his pockets. He addressed his answer to Maggie's question directly to me. "We'll put her in intensive care for a while – put her in a bigger pot and let her roots gain strength. At least six months, maybe more – maybe a lot more. Then we'll plant her in the hospital healing garden, out on the island. There's a place out there for a tree, you know, and I been waiting for just the right one." He angled his head toward the healing tree. "She just might be the one."

"Do you think she'll make it?" Maggie plucked a dead leaf from a branch. Jerry again addressed his response to me. "Hard telling. It's gonna take some special care. But a tree's like a person, you know. Never beyond helping and never beyond hoping. And never beyond caring. No guarantees, of course, but I do believe she'll do just fine out there in the garden."

Jerry took the healing tree with him to the intensive care unit for sick trees. Maggie went to deliver a poem to a newly-diagnosed cancer patient. It was still raining outside, more heavily than before. The heater clicked on, and the breeze from the vent blew one last dead sycamore tree leaf from the windowsill onto the floor. "What's the point," I asked of no one in particular. "God's busy elsewhere."

FAST FORWARD TO THE PAST

I am glorying in this second childhood
Once again my head is fuzzy
    On the outside and on the inside

I spit up a lot but don't let it get me down
I've got really big dreams but an awfully short memory
And I tend to not look very far ahead

I don't want much
    But what I do want
        I want right now

I'm easy to please and quick to forgive
    I'll share anything with anyone
        Whether it's mine or not

I'd give you all the gold in Fort Knox
    For an afternoon in the back yard
        With a brand new puppy

Then I'd invite you to put away your treasure and
Come out back to play with us

                    Maggie Mermaid

Chapter Sixteen

"Have you gotten the reality speech yet?" Maggie was perched in my wheelchair. I was propped up in my bed.

"The reality speech?"

"Yeah. The one where they tell you that you're in denial, that sooner or later you're going to have to accept the reality of your situation."

"You mean the one that goes, 'You're never going to walk again, so deal with it'?"

"Yeah. Or the one that goes, 'You're 26 years old. Don't you think it's time for you to make up a will? Like, real soon?' That one."

It took a moment for Maggie's words to sink in. "What do you mean, Maggie? Have you gotten that speech?"

Maggie pulled her knees up to her chest and I had the sudden panicky notion that this change in her center of gravity might tip the wheelchair over backwards. "What do you mean, Maggie? What have they told you?" My overprotective Momma glands had just kicked into high gear.

Maggie shrugged and laid her chin on her knees. "That I should make up my will. More or less." She looked out the window, then back at me. "But they're wrong. I mean, I'll probably outlive all of them." *A mermaid in a riptide, desperately clutching at an invisible anchor.* "Oh, Maggie." That's all I could say.

"Don't worry." She looked out the window and smiled, and I had the sudden overwhelming impression that she was looking out at a choir of angels who were at that very moment looking in at her. "They've told me that before, and I've always proved them wrong. And they're wrong again this time. But, just in case, I did do a will." She looked over at me with a frail smile. "I'll be leaving you my pink journal. In case, you know, I don't fill it all up. You can, like, finish it for me." She returned her gaze to the window and the angels beyond. They were, I knew, calling to her.

"It's going to be okay, Carrie Anne. Whatever happens, it's going to be okay. I mean, how many girls get to live their dreams – get to spend their days writing poems for people who really appreciate getting them? My life has been blessed. Every minute is a blessing, whether I have one or a million of them left. It's going to be okay."

I closed my eyes and visualized myself getting up out of this bed and walking over to the window and closing the shades, to stop those wicked angels from calling to Maggie. They couldn't have her. Not yet. Not for a long time. "It's going to be a while before I'm confident enough to write in your pink journal, Maggie, so you'd better stick around." I crossed my arms and set my jaw firm to let those wicked death angels know they'd have a fight on their hands if they came through the glass.

Maggie smiled but there were no dancing leprechauns in her eyes. "That's not going to be my decision, Carrie Anne. Some of us are born to be summer flowers." She opened her journal and thumbed through it until she found the page she was looking for. "Some things, I don't know how to talk about except by doing it in verse." She looked at her poem, then back at me. "Want to hear?" I knew that if I tried to say anything I'd cry, so I just bit my lip and nodded. She stared into the pink journal for a silent moment. The she read:

I am afraid…

Afraid of the pain

    I even now can't endure;

That I know will grow worse

    from both the disease and the cure.

Dear God, did you have to give me this pain?

What's in it for you, and for me what's the gain?

I am afraid…

Afraid of the loneliness

    when old friends disappear;

They avoid me like death;

    what is it they fear?

Dear God, now I need a comforting hand.

Why is it my friends just don't understand?

I am afraid…

Afraid of my dying,

    and not knowing what's next.

Am I destined for heaven?

    Did I pass the big test?

Dear God, I don't want death, there's so much left to do.

Why must my life end with my work still not through?

I am afraid…

Afraid of the fear

    I face new every day.

It's destroying my soul

    As my life ebbs away.

Dear God, it's the fear that tortures me worst.

Where's the peace you promised would soothe all my hurts?

I am afraid…

Afraid that I won't have the courage to die.

Afraid there's no heaven beyond the blue sky.

Afraid of my suffering, that there's no reason why.

Dear God, it's the fear that keeps me from you.

In this terrible dark valley, please see me through.

Maggie closed the cover of the pink journal the way a grieving parent might close the lid on a child's casket. "I was diagnosed with cancer when I was fifteen. In an earlier day, I wouldn't have seen my sixteenth birthday." Maggie smiled and now there was a bit of the old impishness in her emerald eyes. "Robbie would have had to find another chauffer because I never would have gotten old enough to get a driver's license. I prayed for a miracle, and the people of this hospital gave me one. More than one. Now I'm praying for another miracle, but whether I get it or not, I'm pretty darned lucky to have had the last ten years. I wouldn't trade the experiences that my cancer has given me, or the people I've met along the journey, for ten thousand years without cancer."

The realization hit me like an oversized wave crashing onto the beach just how much I'd been leaning on Maggie to help me cope with the loss of Mark. I wanted a hurricane to blow away those terrible angels waiting outside the window. Maggie was at peace, it seemed, but I wanted to rage and rage against the dying of her light.

"Dylan Thomas didn't write that poem for his father, Carrie Anne," she said, somehow having read my thoughts. "He wrote it for himself. Because he wasn't ready to let go. But we have to. The doctors and the nurses, they're doing everything they can. It's not in our hands anymore. We have to let go."

I didn't cry until after Maggie left. Then I raged and I raged through a bleak night that was anything but gentle.

BE CAREFUL WHAT YOU PRAY FOR

I prayed for wealth

    was given more work

I prayed for strength

    was called to exercise

I prayed for peace

    was told to serve

I prayed for wisdom

    was shown the library

I prayed for generalities

    was answered with specifics

C.A.M.

Chapter Seventeen

"One more try." I'd spent the past twenty minutes immobilized and crying, and now Amanda was telling me to try again. A year ago, Mark and I had hiked to the top of Long's Peak in Colorado, and now I couldn't even pull myself from the wheelchair onto a hospital bed. "Just one more try, Carrie Anne, then I'll take you back."

"I can't." I started to cry again, only this time more from self-pity than from frustration. "I can't." Every day, it was the same thing. Amanda or one of the other physical therapists would take me down to the gym and then tell me to do something impossible. *Pull yourself onto the bed, Carrie Anne. Turn yourself into a fish, Carrie Anne.*

Amanda stepped behind the wheelchair and hooked her forearms under my armpits, lifting gently. "Come on, Carrie Anne. Grab onto the bedrails and pull. You're going to have to master this before you can go back home. Before you can live on your own again."

Live on my own? As in without Mark? I made another half-hearted attempt, then gave in to self-pity and collapsed back into the chair. "I can't," I whispered. "Please, just take me back to my room. I can't do this."

Amanda walked around to the side and nudged one of those big rubber exercise balls in my direction. She sat on it, keeping her balance as easily as an ordinary person sitting in an ordinary chair, and I was envious beyond reason. She stared at me for a moment (I avoided her gaze by looking at my knees), then said, "That word is poison, Carrie Anne, that word 'can't.' Even when it's accurate, it's usually not true."

"How can something be accurate but not true?"

"It is accurate that right now, you seem to be unable to pull yourself up onto that bed, but it is not true that you can't do it. The real truth is that you really *can* do this. But when you add the letter T to the end of the word can, it's like putting an umbrella over a picnic table. It prevents the sunshine of possibility from shining in. Every time you cover 'can' with T and turn it into 'can't' you're quitting before you've even tried."

"But I really can't." I slapped the sides of my legs. "These legs really are dead, and all the positive thinking in the world's not going to make them jump."

"Well, maybe not." Amanda was still giving me the stare that I could not return. "But I've seen miracles happen before, and I'm not going to rule one out for you, not as quickly as you seem to have."

"Humph. God's not going to raise Mark from the dead, and God's not going to breathe life back into these legs. He's busy elsewhere."

"Okay," Amanda said, "maybe you never will walk again. In fact, you probably won't. I'll give you that. So why don't you start thinking about what you still can do?"

Defiance came back with a vengeance. I was not going to let go of the self-pity tar baby that easily. "Well, in case you didn't know, Amanda, mountain trails are not handicapped accessible." Hiking through the mountains with Mark had been much on my mind, and in my dreams, in recent days. "And I somehow can't see myself clamping my wheelchair onto a ski lift."

Amanda looked at me the way a rattlesnake might regard a mouse. "Listen Carrie Anne. Every winter I take a handicapped accessible van full of people in wheelchairs to the mountains to go skiing. Some of them, I have a hard time keeping up with on the way down. You want to know what the difference is between them and you?"

At that moment, I did not want to know the difference between me and Amanda's ski bums, and made sure my body language sent the message. She told me anyway. "They're survivors. Same circumstances you have, only a different way of looking at them." Amanda's expression never changed, she just sat there on rocking on her ball staring at me. At last, she asked me a question. "Would you like to hear the one simple word that will transform you from being a victim into being a survivor?"

Oh gawd, another one word that's going to change my life. "Go ahead," I replied, wiping my nose and eyes on my sleeve, since there weren't any Kleenex handy, and Amanda didn't seem to be overly concerned about getting some for me, "tell me the word that's going to change my life."

"Yet."

"Yet?"

"Yep. As soon as you add 'yet' to the words 'I can't,' your mental focus will shift from the past to the future. I said I've seen miracles happen, and I have. And every single one of them had its roots in acceptance – acceptance of what has happened. Yeah, it was a tragic thing, that accident. But it happened. It's not going to un-happen. So life goes on – or not – when you start thinking about what you still can do and stop whining about what you can no longer do."

"Is this another tough love speech?"

"Don't you think you need it?" Amanda replied without smiling.

I nodded. "I suppose so."

"Every time you hear yourself uttering those toxic and disempowering words – I can't – you just tack on the word yet.

Like, I can't pull myself onto this bed – yet. Like, I can't go to the mountains – yet. Like, I can't live a normal life – yet." Amanda was rolling her exercise ball back and forth like a seal in the circus. "Think about it," she went on. "The word yet is only one letter removed from the word yes. Add 'yet' to 'I can't' and you change your focus from the past – all the dead weight that's holding you back – to the future – the things you must do in order to move forward. 'I can't yet' is just another way of saying 'I can, but first I need to…' and then filling in the blank. You go ahead and do whatever it is that's in that blank, and you'll move yourself one step closer to removing the T from the end of can. And eventually, you might even change No to Yes. Do that, and someday I'll be telling some other patient about a miracle patient named Carrie Anne Murphy."

"So that's my prescription? Say yet, and expect a miracle?"

Amanda finally smiled. "That's your prescription. Add yet to can't, work hard, and expect a miracle. Just don't give God a deadline."

As the transport aide pushed me back to the rehab unit, I was almost afraid to look up for fear of seeing that umbrella of impossibility towering above my wheelchair, blocking out the sun of potential. I wanted to be strong, to take one magnificent breath and blow that umbrella away forever. I also knew that when it came to escaping the shadow, there would be no "forever." It would be day by day, every day, one day at a time, for the rest of my life.

The windows in the rehab unit patient rooms went down almost all the way to the floor so that people in wheelchairs could see the world outside. From my room I could look down on the healing garden. The healing tree was still in Jerry's arboreal intensive care unit, but I somehow knew that someday she would be thriving out there on her own little island, a beacon of hope for the patients of Memorial Hospital. I let my mind wander off to the mountains. When we were both retired, Mark and I had planned to live in a little log home somewhere in the Rockies. We loved hiking and we loved skiing. I thought about

Amanda's bus for crippled ski bums and tried to picture myself there, riding toward the mountains. I knew they had special ski chairs for paraplegics like me. Also knew I'd never have the courage to try it. *"Never?" Is that a variation on the "I can't" theme?* It was the voice of Amanda in my head. Could I really do it? Could I really face down my fears and ski down a mountain slope knowing that the legs underneath me were as cold and dead as the snow on the ground? I wheeled myself over to the table and started to write:

COURAGE

Ostrich sticks his neck out

Head down in the sand

Eyes squeezed tightly shut

Thinks the view is grand

Giraffe surveys the landscape

Head up in a tree

Knows you have to take some risk

If you're truly to be free

I wheeled myself back over to the window and sat there with my eyes closed. In my imagination I could see Jerry Landerall rowing a little boat across the pond toward the island. And the healing tree was in the boat with him.

Chapter Eighteen

The next day, Amada wasn't able to get me to pull myself up onto the bed, though I did manage to tip over the wheelchair once – a mishap she seemed to regard as a major milestone. When she got me back to my room, I told her I never wanted to see the physical therapy gym again, but at least this time I laughed when I said it. After she left, I wheeled myself over to the window so I could watch the sunset (and pray for the type of miracle you don't have to work or wait for).

It was dark when Abby, the evening shift nurse who brought me milkshakes when I couldn't bring myself to eat real food (a trick I'd learned from Maggie), gently shook my shoulder. "Sorry to wake you up, Carrie Anne, but I knew you'd want me to."

It took a moment for me to remember that I was sitting alone in my wheelchair in a hospital room in the real world, and not laying on a bearskin rug with Mark in front of a fireplace in the log cabin of my dream world. "Sure, Abby, no problem. What is it?"

She'd already unlocked the wheels and was pushing me past my bed toward the door. "I think you need to see Maggie. She's having a rough night. They called over from Oncology and said she's been asking for you." We were out in the long corridor that connects the rehab unit with the rest of the hospital, wheeling along quickly and quietly. Amanda's three letter word "yet" kept running through my mind, but in a new context. *Not yet, God, not yet. You can't take Maggie yet.*

When Abby pushed me into the unit, the nurse behind the counter nodded at her without smiling, and without looking at me. *This is going to be bad.* Moving much more slowly now, Abby pushed me down the hall. A housekeeper I recognized as one of Maggie's friends was coming out of her room. She was crying. *Really bad.*

Abby stopped at the door to Maggie's room. "Let me just go in and make sure she's ready for you." She touched my shoulder on the way past. When she came back out, I could tell that she, too, was losing the fight to hold back her tears. "Brace yourself," she whispered, then wheeled me through the door. No amount of bracing could have prepared me to see Maggie like this – a baby bird fallen from her nest, a helpless mermaid being circled by remorseless sharks.

"You stay for as long as you want," Abby whispered as she parked my wheelchair next to Maggie's bed. She dimmed the lights further on her way out, and I knew that before she returned to rehab, she'd rig up some sort of do not disturb sign on the door. Maggie's eyes were closed, and the imperceptible rise and fall of her chest couldn't have been moving enough air to keep a baby parakeet alive.

"Hi, Maggie." I reached out and touched her forehead. Her head lolled to the side and she opened her eyes, though she was looking at me from a place far away from this cancer ward. She smiled thinly and tried to say something, but I couldn't make it out. I shrugged, shook my head and leaned closer. "Say it again, Maggie. I couldn't hear you."

She rested for a while, and I feared that she'd fallen asleep for the last time. After a long time, she opened her eyes again and mouthed the words. "Write me a poem."

Her pink journal was lying open on the bedside table, her favorite fat pen resting in the crease – a torch, waiting to be passed. I'd been running away from that torch since the ninth grade, and now the irrational thought came into my head that if I kept running, Maggie couldn't die, because she would have to carry it. Someone had to, right?

"I can't, Maggie. I'm not a real poet like you are. I'm not a mermaid." I passed my hand through the bedrail and reached under the sheets. Her hand was skin and bone. And it was on fire. Even though I could see her and hear her and touch her, I was losing her. *Oh No!*

Maggie opened her eyes again, and there was still the faintest glimmer of the emerald fire in them. "Yes you can," she whispered. In the years to come, I would hear the invisible whisper of those three words a million times – as they wheeled me out of my hospital cocoon to finally take me home; the day I drove my new car that was specially-equipped with paraplegic controls; as Amanda buckled me into the custom ski that reignited my passion for the sport Mark and I had loved so well; the day I wheeled myself into the hospital volunteer office and clipped on my new nametag: *Carrie Anne Murphy – Poetry Therapist.* But on this day, I was powerless to do the one thing I would have given anything to be able to do. I was losing Maggie.

Write me a poem. She didn't need to speak. I heard it in her eyes.

I closed my eyes and prayed. *God, please give me a poem. A poem for Maggie. And make it a good one.* When God didn't answer, I knew I'd be on my own. After drawing a few doodles, I finally scribbled down the first poem I would write in my new capacity as apprentice poetry therapist, the first poem I would ever write in what was to become my pink journal. But it was not a poem for Maggie. It was a poem for me:

> Maggie Maggie all alone
>
> Heart of gold in a world of stone
>
> You make me laugh
>
> You make me cry
>
> Maggie Maggie please don't die

When you're ready, the poem you need will find you. How many times had Maggie said that? I smiled to remember that she'd also said to not worry about your poem finding the Pulitzer Prize committee, because that's not who it was for. I started to read my poem aloud, but then realized I didn't need to. Maggie could read it from where she was.

I closed the pink journal and replaced it on the bedside table. Then I grabbed the side rail of Maggie's bed with both hands and started to rock myself forward, the way Amanda had showed me. On the last forward lunge I shoved with all the strength I had. As my weight centered over the bed rail, I forced my arms out straight and twisted myself at the waist. Lurching forward, my head crashed into Maggie's pillow, face down. Though I couldn't feel them, I knew that my legs still dangled over the bed rails.

I struggled to get my face out of the pillow, then to pull my legs onto the bed. After catching my breath, I turned to Maggie, my nose touching her cheek. "I wrote you a poem, Maggie."

You know, there just aren't enough words in the English language. Somewhere between "I love hot dogs" and "I love my husband" there needs to be a better way to say "I love Maggie."

Maggie never opened her eyes, but there was the slightest hint of a smile. It was the smile of a mermaid who, having finished her work on land, was now ready to rejoin her sisters in the sea.

AFTERLIFE

Every particle in every body was born at the same second
With the exploding of an infinitely tiny Nothing
Into an infinitely expanding Something
Since the beginning of time
Nothing new has been created
Nothing old has been destroyed
> In the truest sense of the word
> You were never born
> You cannot die
You can only be rearranged

C.A.M.

Chapter Nineteen

Not even on his third day inside the belly of the great fish could Jonah have been in a darker or more miserable place than I was right now, once again back on my back in a hospital bed. They'd sent me from the rehab unit back to the general hospital for another operation. Mark had deserted even my dreams, Maggie was dead, Robbie was on an Outward Bound adventure, and I was recuperating from this latest round of surgery. Maggie's prescription for depression was to write yourself out of it, but when I tried, I only dug myself deeper down into the abyss. Even the little squiggle of a mermaid I tried to draw in Maggie's memory looked more like a dead fish rotting on the beach than a finned angel cruising the ocean deeps.

"Happy poems don't win prizes," Maggie once told me. Now there was a thought. I read over my latest funeratorio and patted myself on the back (figuratively speaking, of course). Maybe they'd give this one a prize after all (posthumously, of course). Here was something worthy of Plath or Sexton or Teasdale or one of those other women poets who had taken their own lives, after having written so many poems alerting their readers that they *really were* going to do it, by and by. A poem short and bitter, befitting the fate of a woman come late to poetry and destined to die young, so I thought.

RESTING IN PEACE

I once was afraid of the dark
Of legion black molecules snaking
Into my body through every orifice
Freezing me in a coagulate of despair

I once was afraid of solitude
Of talking to the air and hearing no
Echo in reply to reaffirm my body and
Reify my existence

I once was afraid of confinement
Of tiny rooms where you can reach
Out and touch every wall and
Rub your nose on the velvet

I once was afraid of sleeping
Of the nightmare world more real
Than the flowers in a graveyard
That holds you petrified against your will

I once was afraid of infinity
Of the distant reaches where space and
Time interpenetrate like a fertilized egg
In the womb of God

I once was afraid in the dark
Alone in a small room
Asleep
Forever

The sun must have been setting outside, though you couldn't tell through the gray curtain of autumn rain. My legs, the part of my body where pain would have been a welcome sign of progress, remained in a novocained deep freeze; from my waist up, though, I felt like a lava lamp, with hot globules of pain coursing through my body. Maggie had also said that poets wrote their best poems when they were in pain. So rather than waste the metaphor, I picked up the pen and started to scribble again.

Let's see. Death Valley. Dead Sea. Dead Drunk, Dead Duck. Dead Serious, Dead Broke, Dead Wrong. Dead Eye. Dead End. As the words came, I actually began to wish I could write myself into a coffin. That's when Maggie took matters into her own hands. There could be no other explanation for the train of events that transpired over the next several hours. It started with the singing in the hallway. Lestelle, the housekeeper I'd seen coming out of Maggie's room in tears on that sad night, had parked her cleaning cart outside my room and was softly singing a gospel song. Not just any song, mind you – the one that had touched my soul since I'd first heard it as a little girl. But not with the words I'd grown up with. Lestelle made up her own lyrics and was (I now know) singing them for me – to me, from Maggie:

> Amazing Grace, now Maggie's home
>
> She's looking down on me
>
> She gives me comfort through the pain
>
> And sets my spirit free

I closed my eyes and allowed myself to fall into the song, and as I did the pain actually did seem to recede. The last words reverberated in my head, like an echo fading into the depths of a slot canyon. *Now Maggie's home at last.* I expected to hear a bring-the-house-down ovation, but there was just the silence of a hospital ward in the evening hours, and Lestelle working quietly at her cart.

And then… the most extravagant wolf whistle I've ever heard. Opening my eyes, I looked out into the corridor. Lestelle was obviously happy to see whoever was coming down the hall. "Well, look'a here – it's Mistuh Rufus Maximus!" I'd heard rumors of Rufus, the talking parrot who was part of the hospital's pet therapy program, but had never seen him myself.

A distinguished-looking older gentleman in one of those blue blazers that hospital volunteers wear came into view and stopped to talk with Lestelle. He had a parrot on his shoulder, pirate style, which I surmised to be Mistuh Rufus Maximus. The bird looked through the open door into my room and did another wolf whistle. The volunteer glanced at me, then looked at his bird. "What's that you say, Rufus? You want to meet the pretty lady in that room?" The bird whistled again. The volunteer said goodbye to Lestelle and stuck his head in my door. "Good evening. I'm Peter Graves, and this is Rufus. We're volunteers. Rufus is usually quite shy, but he's asked if he could meet you." Rufus was marching in place on Peter's shoulder. I shrugged. *Why not?*

Peter walked in. Rufus whistled, then squawked, "Hi, Cutie!"

"Now Rufus," Peter said, "don't be too forward. You'll scare her off." Rufus marched and flapped his wings. Peter stepped over to the side of the bed. "Rufus is an African gray parrot. They're the smartest birds in the world, you know." Rufus nodded his agreement, and Peter laughed. "They're also not the least bit humble about it." Rufus whistled once more. "Hi, Cutie!"

I smiled despite myself. Other than Mark, no one had called me Cutie since Robbie was a toddler. Not even the plastic surgeon who'd patched up my face, and you'd have thought that was part of his job description. Peter lifted Rufus from his shoulder onto his hand, then held the bird in front of his face and asked, "What's that you say?" Rufus squawked a reply. "Well, old chap," Peter said, "that's awfully bold of you. But I'll ask her."

Peter looked down at me. "Rufus was wondering if he might perch on your hand for a bit."

"On my hand? Well, I don't know. I've never held a live bird before." Rufus whistled and spread his wings. Peter laughed again. "Rufus says that previous experience is not required." Rufus marched impatiently as Peter showed me how to position my hand, then made the transfer. The bird turned out to be much lighter than I thought he'd be. "Hello, pretty bird." Rufus cocked his head to the side and made a clucking noise, the way an old man sitting at a sidewalk coffee shop might try to draw the attention of a pretty young girl passing by. "What else does one say to an African gray parrot?" I asked Peter.

"Whatever's on your mind. He is, after all, a member in good standing of the hospital's pet therapy program. A therapist, you see, in his own right. Just be aware that whatever you do say is likely to be repeated."

I brought Rufus up closer to my face. He leaned forward and gave my nose a gentle peck. "Rufus!" Peter scolded. "On the first date, a gentleman waits until the end of the evening for his kiss. Where are your manners?"

Rufus marched in place on my hand and gave me another wolf whistle. "Hi, Cutie!"

"Rufus," humphed Peter, "you are hopeless!"

Rufus suddenly stood dead still and stared at me, the inquisitive gaze of a two-year-old at the zoo upon first seeing a giraffe. There was something so very human in that bird's eyes. I swear he actually cleared his throat before speaking his next words. "Hell-ooooooo..." He hung onto the note like a soprano at the opera. Then... "Maaaaaggie." There was no mistaking what he'd said. I blinked hard. Rufus whistled again.

Peter shook his head sadly. "Rufus loves everybody, but Maggie was his favorite. He still misses her." Rufus nodded in agreement. "Hell-ooooooo Maaaaaggie." Rufus gripped my hand for balance, leaned forward, and squawked out these words: "You can." Clear as a bell. Then he gave my nose another gentle peck.

"Well, well, well. Where did that come from, Master Maximus?" Peter looked at me and said, "Rufus knows seventy-two words, but I've never heard him say that before. 'You can.' He must have learned it specially for you." Rufus nodded even more fervently than before. "Hell-oooooo Maaaaaggie."

Hello Maggie? Or was it hello *from* Maggie? I'd never know for sure. Not in this lifetime, anyway. But there was no doubt in my mind that had Maggie been able to deliver one single message to me through this little winged therapist, those would have been her words. *You can, Carrie Anne. Yes you can.*

Chapter Twenty

Peter and Rufus had left, but Maggie (I'm sure this was all Maggie's doing) wasn't done yet. I was sitting up in the bed with the pink journal open on my lap, trying (not very hard) to not fall back into the self-pity I'd been wallowing around in before their visit. I wanted to write a poem about Maggie and Rufus, pretty birds up in a tree – but this is what came out:

PRETTY BIRD

Tiny yellow goldfinch lying –

      Dead on –

The side of the road.

Why is it that only the –

      Pretty birds break –

Our hearts by their dying?

"May I come in?" I recognized the man at the door as being one of the hospital chaplains, though I did not know his name. I shrugged in a way intended to say "Go away," but that evidently conveyed "Sure, why not." And in he came.

"Hi, Carrie Anne, I'm Andy Brennan, one of the volunteer chaplains here at the hospital. I'm sorry it's taken me so long to come up, but your request somehow ended up under a pile of papers on my desk, and I just saw it this afternoon."

"My request?"

"Yes. It's our policy. We only visit patients who've requested it."

I shook my head. "I didn't request any visits."

Andy cocked his head to the side and shot me a quizzical look. "Carrie Anne Murphy?" I couldn't very well deny that, not even to get rid of a pesky priest, so I nodded. He rifled through some papers on his clipboard, and when he found what he was looking for, put it on top and showed it to me. Sure enough, my name was on the visitation request. As was a squiggly little mermaid swimming across the top of the page.

I could just picture Maggie up there in heaven, those green eyes all a-twinkle, quite pleased with herself for having this *keep Carrie Anne from getting depressed club* of hers carrying on the effort. I handed the clipboard back. "Well, my brain's been in a fog since the surgery. I guess I forgot about making this request. But thanks for coming up."

He set the clipboard down on the bedside table and put his hands in his pockets. "It's my pleasure. That's what I'm here for." We endured the awkward silence for a moment, then he said, "Here's what I mean by that. I'm here because it's not just the body that needs care in times of trouble; we also need to tend to our spiritual beings. That's where, hopefully, I might be able to help."

"You're not going to give me that 'patience of Job' speech, are you?"

Andy smiled and shook his head, then pulled up a chair and sat where I could see him without having to twist my neck. "No, I'm not going to give you that speech. For one thing, anyone who's actually read the book of Job appreciates that Job was *not* a patient man. Faithful, yes. But Job was angry and anguished and anything but patient. If you're interested, I'll tell you something about the book of Job I think you'll find helpful. After all, like you, Job lost both his health and members of his family."

"Yeah, but unlike me, Job got it all back." I started thumbing through the pink journal, hoping that Andy would take the hint and excuse himself. He didn't.

"You say that as if the final chapter of your story has been written, Carrie Anne." I didn't reply, and Andy let the silence hang in the air. At last he said, "You know, I'm pretty certain that in the months after he lost both his family and his health, Job didn't see any path leading to a bright future either. How could he? How could anyone? But he kept walking, and eventually the path made itself visible. That path brought Job to a new place, but it could not bring back what he had lost. In time, God blessed Job with a new family, but God could not erase the grief that Job would always carry from the loss of his first family."

"So what's that got to do with me?"

Andy shrugged. "As with most stories, it pretty much means what you want it to mean. But here's what I think. While God cannot replace what you've lost, God can show you a new path, a path that will lead you to a wonderful place, perhaps a place you didn't even know you wanted to go to, a place you didn't know existed."

"Yeah, well, it's been several thousand years since anyone's seen God come out of a whirlwind. He's probably busy elsewhere. I think he must have lost interest or something. I'm certainly not banking on any such thing."

Andy laughed. "Neither am I. I'd probably have a heart attack, to see God up close and personal! Frankly, I think God is more subtle than that. And there *is* a very subtle message buried in the book of Job, a message that's often overlooked. It's a message that just might help make your path visible."

He leaned back in his chair and just sat there. Finally, I said, "Well, are you going to tell me what the message is?"

"I will, but I'm not sure you're ready to hear it."

I looked up at the fake clouds that would never blow away. *Why do men have to be so obtuse?* "Well, we won't know that until I hear it, now, will we?" I penciled a note into Maggie's pink journal (I would always think of it as Maggie's pink journal) reminding me to write a poem about how every obtuse man needs an acute woman to keep him on track, then gave Andy my best *okay, buster, show me what you've got* smile.

"As you've just alluded, God came to Job out of the whirlwind and confronted him with his ignorance. And, as you can imagine, Job was terrified. But then God did something else, something you absolutely would not have predicted from the imperious speech that went on before. He instructed Job to pray for the friends who had accused him falsely. And the Bible is very specific in saying that it was *after* Job prayed for his friends that his health and wealth were restored and his family replaced. That's the punch line, if you will."

I shook my head. "I don't get it."

"If you consider the story of Job to be a metaphor, which I do, then that's the most important lesson. Job was made whole when he stopped obsessing over his own problems and instead prayed for someone else. I don't believe that God made a bet with the devil, using Job's family, his health, and his possessions as chips on a celestial gambling table to be sacrificed in a test of Job's faith. What kind of a god would do that? But I *do* believe that God was there for Job in his hour of darkest need. And God will be there for you, giving you strength when you are in need."

Andy stood up and placed his clipboard under his arm. "I spend a lot of time working with support groups, Carrie Anne. And I always find that whatever problems people are faced with – addiction, cancer, whatever – the ones who can at least for a moment set their own problems aside and pray for others, in whatever way they pray, find the greatest measure of healing for themselves. *That* is the message of Job, I believe. Something to think about, isn't it?"

Andy left, but the questions remained. And they multiplied. The notion of making a bet with the devil struck my fancy.

Would God really have made a bet with the devil to test Job's faith? Would Job still have passed that test had he known the whole truth – that it was God himself who gave Satan the go-ahead to slaughter Job's family and servants and to break his body? Just to test his faith? Where was God before he showed up in the whirlwind? Where is God now? Busy elsewhere? Still hobnobbing about with Satan? Had Mark and I somehow unwittingly made, and lost, a bet with the devil the night we thought we were going out to dinner but instead ran smack into a drunk driver who at that very moment might also have been losing his own bet with the devil? I opened the pink journal to the next blank page and started to write.

CASTLES IN THE SAND

The devil and I sat together on the beach

watching the children build castles in the sand

and he, being a betting man, said...

I'll bet you a dollar the next wave knocks them down

and I, being in my bathing suit, said...

I would, but I don't have a dollar with me

and he, being in a generous frame of mind, said...

I'll lend you a dollar if you should lose

and I, feeling particularly lucky, said...

You're on.

How was I to know that three hours ago

that sly devil had dropped a big stone into the water

far out on the ocean, at just the right spot

to cause an unusually large wave to hit the beach

at just the next moment

toppling over the sand castles

and washing the children out to sea?

You owe me a dollar, said the devil, and I, said he,

being the devil, am reneging on my previous offer

of a loan…

But if you're unable to pay in cash, I'm sure

other arrangements can be made.

No, I decided as I reread my poem, Andy was right. God wasn't responsible for Job's tragedy, or mine. But God *was* standing there beside Job as he struggled to cope with it. And though God might not appear out of a windstorm for me, I knew that Andy had been right in saying that God would help me to bear that which otherwise would have been unbearable; that God might help me find a new path, since the old path was forever closed to me. But first I had to pray for my friends.

Chapter Twenty One

I opened the pink journal and closed my eyes. Then I started to think about all the people I could pray for. I started with Robbie, and prayed that he would make a good doctor and a good father – and that he would never make a bet with the devil. Then I prayed for Maggie, that she was safely in heaven writing poems for all the other angels and mermaids. Then I prayed for Mark. And I got stuck there. God was not going to come to me from out of any whirlwind, and God was not going to bring Mark back into my life. He was busy elsewhere.

That was my state of mind when the new nurse came in making the final rounds of the evening. Her name was Evelyn – I could see that from her nametag – but I didn't recall having seen her before. She carried one of those blue plastic trays with the usual assortment of cups and pills.

"Tough night?" She walked over and set the medication tray on the overbed table, then sat down on the edge of the bed. She pulled several Kleenex out of her pocket, used one to dry off my eyes, and placed the rest of them in my hand. I hadn't even realized I'd been crying.

We sat like that for a few moments before I finally said, "One of the hospital chaplains stopped by tonight. Andy… Andy…"

"Andy Brennan?"

"Yes. He was trying to be helpful, but I'm afraid I wasn't very receptive. Or very appreciative. If you get a chance, could you thank him for me?"

"Sure, no problem. I'll make a point of it." She pulled a little pad out of her pocket and made a note. "How's Robbie doing?"

"Uhm, he's doing just fine. How do you know Robbie?"

Evelyn laughed. "Everyone around here has gotten to know Robbie. You don't remember me, but I was one of your nurses when you were first admitted. I've been filling in on another unit. Robbie is quite an exceptional young man. I know this is hard on you both, but I don't think you need to worry about your son."

"I know," I said, thankful for the handful of Kleenex.

Evelyn picked up the book I'd been reading from the overbed table. "Emily Dickinson. I've never read much poetry, but I do remember the one where she compared hope to a bird. Or something like that."

I nodded at the book. "It's one of the dog-eared pages."

She thumbed through the pages and laughed. Almost every page had a bent-down corner. "Would you like me to read to you? A few of your favorites?"

Poems are meant to be heard, not just read. Maggie had told me that was why she always read her poems out loud before giving them to the recipient. I shook my head no. "That's really nice of you to offer, Evelyn, but I know how busy you are. I don't want to take too much of your time."

Evelyn continued thumbing through the book. "Whenever I'm faced with competing demands on my time, I ask this question: What would Florence do? Florence Nightingale founded the profession of nursing. She's my role model. And I think that tonight, Florence would have stopped to read Emily Dickinson for her patient."

I nodded toward the blue plastic tray full of pills. "What about all your other patients?"

Evelyn laughed again. "They aren't going anywhere, and frankly most of them will be perfectly happy to have an extra fifteen minutes before I shove pills down their throats." She looked up at the clock – it was 7:15 – then back at me. "One of my professors at the nursing college shared a secret that has stood me very well: Slow down on the inside and you can speed up on the outside."

"Sounds profound. What does it mean?"

"I think of it as the Principle of the Deep Breath. When I slow down and ask what Florence would do, it seems like I end up getting even more done. That's because it helps me stay focused on what really matters, on what's really important. Most of us have a lot more time than we'll admit to, if we would just pay better attention to how we use it. That's slowing down on the inside so you can speed up on the outside."

"Maggie told me that having cancer had been a blessing because it forced her to appreciate the minutes instead of worrying about the years. She said that even though she'd have fewer minutes than she'd once hoped for, she was able to stretch out the minutes she did have, and pack more into each one of them. I suppose that's the same thing, isn't it?"

"Yes, I suppose that's the same thing." Evelyn was leafing through the Emily Dickinson book. "Now, here's a good one: *If I can ease one life the aching, or cool one pain, I shall not live in vain.* That could be a nurse's credo, couldn't it?" She turned a few more pages, then said, "Wow! What do you suppose she means by this: *A timid thing to drop a life into the purple well.* Purple? Isn't purple the color of depression? I wish I could get that one across to some of my patients, who seem to have given up on themselves, already dropped their lives into that purple well."

Evelyn skimmed through the pages. "I've always thought poetry was, well, boring, you know, sort of priggish stuff. But this is pretty cool. Want me to read you a few?"

"Sure," I replied, "that would be nice. But I don't want you to get in trouble. I mean, reading poetry isn't in the nurse's job description, is it?"

Evelyn shrugged. "My philosophy has always been to proceed until apprehended. I figure if you're going fast enough, by the time they catch up, you've already done what you set out to do." She turned a few more pages. "Here it is, the hope poem." Marking her place with a Kleenex, she laid the book down on the overbed table. "Before I start, let's give you a little something to help you sleep tonight, okay? Doctor's orders." She handed me a pill and a cup of water. I swallowed the pill, shuddered, and gave Evelyn back the empty cup. Then she started to read:

> Hope is the thing with feathers
>
> That perches in the soul,
>
> And sings the tune without the words,
>
> And never stops at all.

As I drifted off to sleep, Evelyn's voice merged with Maggie's voice, which merged with Emily's voice. I somehow knew that Maggie had picked out the poems for Evelyn to read on this purple evening. And as hope flew be-feathered around my room, Maggie and her mermaid sisters smiled from the other side of the aquarium glass that holds back the universal sea.

A QUESTION FOR JESUS

What did Lazarus have to say
On that famous day when you dragged him
From the beautiful heaven promised the faithful
Back into this brutish existence on earth, where
He would soon have to die one more time?
Did he crawl squawking and blinking from the tomb
Like a newborn ejected from momma's womb
Leaving behind nothing
But memory?

C.A.M.

Chapter Twenty Two

Sitting in the physical therapy department waiting room, waiting for my appointment, I noticed they'd put a new poster up on the wall. It had Leonardo da Vinci's famous cruciform image of a blueprint figure, the one you see in medical offices everywhere that looks like a naked man doing jumping jacks without even mussing his hair. Then, in big bold print, the poster proclaimed:

WE REPAIR THE WORLD'S MOST COMPLEX MACHINE

With that metaphor in mind, I scribbled in the pink journal as I watched people come out of the gym: a teenage girl on crutches, a pot-bellied couch potato shuffling along on wobbly knees, a weekend warrior hobbling out with a cane, a frail little old lady leaning on a walker. And I would have traded places with any one of them if it would have meant I could walk again, or even feel pain in my legs again. The time of my appointment came and went – 5 minutes, then 10 minutes behind schedule. As seems to happen when I'm in a morose mood, the words came quickly, and by the time I was called in for my workout (or more accurately, my work-over), I'd completed a new poem (rather I should say a coupleted collection of clichés).

A MOST COMPLEX MACHINE

I am the world's most complex machine

My heart has been broken, there's a hole in my soul

My feelings are aching, my emotions stone cold

My funny bone is fractured and my

wish bone's been cracked

Bruised is my ego, wounded my pride

My gut issues warnings, my spirit has died

No doctor can fix me

No nurse ease the pain

I'm running on empty

And lost in the rain

Maggie used to say that she'd write her sorrows into the pink journal, then close the covers and leave them inside. More often than not, however, I found that my sorrows seemed to drag me into the journal after them. Thus it was that my self-pity was churning itself into high gear when Amanda came for me. "Sorry to keep you waiting, Carrie Anne, we've been incredibly busy this morning. But now I'm ready for you if you're ready for me."

"I don't really have a choice," I replied, "since the transporter who brought me over won't be back for another hour." At that point, anything sounded better than exercising with Amanda – especially indulging myself in woetry: the poetry of woe. But she just laughed and wheeled me back into the little torture chamber she called her gym.

"Okay, today we're going to start working on your arm strength," Amanda said as she lifted two dumbbells from the farthest end of the weight rack. Laying my hands flat on my lap, she set one dumbbell in each palm and asked me to lift them in a curling motion. They looked like extra-long toothpicks with a marshmallow stuck on each end, but I could barely pick them up.

After a few feeble attempts, I let the dumbbells fall to the floor. They even sounded like marshmallows when they hit. "Look, Amanda," I said, "I've been thinking about this, and I've decided I'm going to get an electric wheelchair. I just don't think I'll ever have the strength to push myself up and down the streets." I tried to cross my arms and was appalled to discover that I was already exhausted by what I'm sure Amanda had assumed would be a light warm-up. "I'll graduate to the manual model when I get stronger."

As she always did when she was about to give me a talking-to, Amanda rolled over the big green exercise ball and sat on it. "This is your decision, Carrie Anne, but please don't make it lightly. Electric wheelchairs can be a life-enhancing resource for people who really need them. But in all my years of physical therapy, I don't know that I've ever seen anyone graduate, as you put it, from an electric to a manual wheelchair."

"So what's wrong with just going electric? Seems a lot easier and more convenient."

Amanda rolled back and forth on her green exercise ball. "Two things. First, now more than ever you need to exercise and keep yourself as strong as possible. If for no other reason, scientists are doing some amazing research on spinal cord injuries. It's possible that, within your lifetime, they'll figure out how to help people walk again. You know as well as I do, the first patients they select will be the ones most likely to do well, and that means those who are strong. No guarantees, of course, but you want to be ready just in case."

"And the second reason?"

"You mean other than just the fact that you'll feel better?" I nodded and she continued. "When you fall into that electric wheelchair lifestyle – and make no mistake, it is a lifestyle – you'll profoundly change the way other people look at you, and place all sorts of restrictions on your own activities."

"What sort of restrictions?"

"Well, for example, people in electric wheelchairs don't ski or participate in marathons."

"Marathons? You've got to be kidding. I can't even wheel myself up the ramp to the main hospital."

"Not yet. Never forget that word 'yet' Carrie Anne. Some of the wheelchair athletes I work with today were once in the same shape you're in now. They had to work hard, and were often tempted to quit, but to a person they'll tell you it was worth the effort."

Before I could respond, the receptionist stepped into the entryway and said, "Amanda, Bill Terry is here to see you, and also Faye Milliken is here for her 11 o'clock appointment."

"Could you please tell Bill I'll be right with him, and go ahead and bring Faye in? Thanks, Shirley."

Faye appeared to be about 16 years old, with a smile that belied the obvious seriousness of her condition. Not only was she in a wheelchair, her head and neck were immobilized by a halo device. Amanda picked up the toothpick-and-marshmallow dumbbells from the floor and handed them to Faye. Then she walked over to the weight rack, picked up the next-larger set, and laid them in my hands. "Faye, this is Carrie Anne. She's going to be your strength coach this morning." Turning to me, Amanda said, "Carrie Anne, could you please start by showing Faye how to do the arm curls, and I'll be right back."

I tried to knock Amanda off her feet with my eyes, but she just laughed and said, "See one, do one, teach one. I'll be back in a bit."

For the next 15 minutes, Faye and I got to know each other. Her neck had been broken when she was thrown from her dirt bike, something she seemed to consider to have been nothing more than a minor speed bump in her life. She would, she assured me, dance with her boyfriend at the senior prom next spring. I'm not sure whether it was from having been put in the position of being someone's coach, or from having a workout buddy, but the new weights somehow seemed lighter than the marshmallow ones that Faye was now using.

When Amanda returned, she was accompanied by a man in a wheelchair. It was one of those little three-wheeled buggy-like things that paraplegics race with. The shoulders peering through his tank-top t-shirt suggested that he was probably pretty good at it. "Carrie Anne and Faye, this is Bill Terry."

After a bit of small talk, Amanda asked Bill to share some of the most important lessons he'd learned about life in a wheelchair. "The first thing I learned is to be careful what you pray for," he said with a hearty laugh. "Fifteen years ago, we were building a custom house and one of our laborers no-showed. So I had to fill in for the deadbeat. The last thing I remember saying to myself was 'Lord, I wish I didn't have to haul this lumber around anymore; I've got more important things to do.' Well, seven minutes later a pile of roofing shingles landed on top of me. I haven't hauled a stick of lumber since that day!" He laughed again, and it was the sound of an icebreaker plowing through a frozen sea.

We talked for over an hour. Amanda canceled the transporter – said she'd wheel me back herself (which I knew really meant she'd try to make me push myself most of the way). Bill shared a few practical strategies for being what he called 'a wheelestrian' in a pedestrian world. But mostly, he spoke about the power of vision. "The book of Proverbs says that without vision, people perish. I know I'd have perished without new dreams to sustain me. I knew I'd never play golf again, so I took up wheelchair racing. Knew I'd never supervise a construction site, so I started my own business. You know, it's funny, but if it hadn't been for that accident, I never would have given myself permission to make a living following my heart's true passion."

"So, what your heart's true passion?" Faye asked the question.

Bill grabbed the rear wheels of his chair and leaned way back so the front wheel was suspended mid-air. Then he tipped to one side and while balanced on just one wheel, spun his wheelchair around in a complete 360-degree circle, then did another, then another. "I'm a wheelchair juggler," he exclaimed while still balancing on one wheel. "The only one in the world, as far as I know."

"You make a living juggling wheelchairs?" Faye asked with a laugh.

Bill remained perfectly balanced on one wheel. "Haven't tried that one yet. But I juggle just about anything else while sitting in a wheelchair. Hammers, bowling balls, peacock feathers, pretty much anything. As far as making a living at it, technically I suppose you'd call me a motivational speaker. But the juggling opens doors into principals' offices and into the hearts and minds of students. First I juggle bowling balls, then I juggle words," he said with another of those icebreaker laughs. After planting all three wheels firmly on the ground (to my great relief) Bill said, "One of the most helpful things I learned was something Amanda taught me: bilateral visualization."

Bill looked over at Amanda, and she took her cue. "I'm a big believer in visualization. Like, if my patient will actually see herself doing an exercise in her mind, she always gets a better performance from her body. But I take that one step further. If I myself also visualize my patient doing the exercise, really doing it right, we get an even greater range of motion. I don't know why it works, but every therapist I know agrees with me that it does work."

Bill nodded. "It's true. When I'm teaching someone to juggle, not only do I ask them to visualize themselves keeping the balls in the air, I also keep that picture in my own mind. It works every time." He looked from me to Faye and back to me. "A few more weeks of weight-lifting, and you'll both be ready for juggling lessons." I don't know if it was the strength of Bill's mind, or the weakness of my own, but in that moment I actually had a mental picture of myself sitting in my wheelchair juggling three tennis balls.

I'd been correct in my assumption that Amanda would try to make me do all the work getting myself back to my room. I made it as far as the ramp that links the medical arts building to the hospital. "Someday I'll be able to do this, Amanda," I said, "but not yet," and we both laughed. She pushed me the rest of the way to my room. Still, it was the farthest I'd ever pushed my wheelchair, and the first time I knew with certainty that someday I *would* power myself up inclines like this. Sitting in my room that afternoon, I rewrote the poem I'd done in the waiting room.

A MOST COMPLEX MACHINE, INDEED!

I am the world's most complex machine

I can be cured by a word

Healed with a touch

Touched by a thought

I use love as a crutch

The things that most matter

You can't really see

It takes invisible tools to fix

The machine that is me

I liked the second one much better.

Chapter Twenty Three

I'd spent the morning in my wheelchair in the sunroom re-reading the poems in Maggie's pink journal, sipping coffee that grew colder page by page. With every line that had been crossed out, rewritten, and crossed out again, I felt her frustration. With every squiggled smiley-faced mermaid signifying that a poem had finally passed the test, I heard her jubilant cackle and smiled along with her.

In these pages I saw the hope and the courage Maggie had shared with so many others whose own hope and courage had deserted them. And I saw the fears she'd kept to herself in poems of hopeless desperation, poems that were written in the depths of endless nights, words written from the eye of the nightmare storm that passes for slumber in the dark hours of one who is facing death. Unlike poems of hope and courage that were drafted, revised, and painstakingly rewritten for others, those she wrote for herself met the page on first draft, as if she wanted to get them out of her head and onto the paper, then turn the page as quickly as possible. No squiggled mermaids celebrated their completion. Turning another page, I saw the last poem that Maggie wrote in her incarnation as an earth-bound mermaid, a poem that would never be read by anyone but me.

And So It Ends...

with neither a bang nor a whimper –
closing the gate, setting the sun,
a sigh, a backward glance, the river bends
disappearing into the mysteries ahead.

I go willing into this gentle night, and
would not trade an eternity of living
for having earned the right to be thus dead.

It broke my heart to think of sweet Maggie, who had never hurt a mosquito or a mayfly, facing those desperate last hours beyond our reach. *Maggie Maggie all alone.* On the right hand side, opposite Maggie's last poem, a weak hand had scrawled two barely legible words. *There's more.* That was all. *There's more.* But there was no more. The remaining pages were blank.

"I left the empty pages for you, Carrie Anne." At some level of consciousness, I knew I was dreaming, that Maggie could not be sitting there in the sunroom with me, asking me to pick up the torch she could no longer carry. But at a deeper level – the level where apparent reality stretches out a tentative finger and touches the real thing – I also knew she *was* sitting right there beside me, and that this would be the last time we'd be together for a long time.

Not wanting to break the spell, I let go of my legs and floated up to the far corner by the window, where the late afternoon sun was warmest. Maggie was perched on the window sill, swinging her legs. She was wearing a t-shirt that said, *If you can read this, you're close enough for a hug.* The broken lady sat motionless in her wheelchair. There was something different about this otherworld Maggie. The nervous energy that had caused her to vibrate like an out-of-balance gyroscope had been replaced by an ethereal calm which suffused the space around her, like the air around the healing tree.

I watched from my perch up by the window as Maggie gave the broken lady a poetry lesson. "Writing a poem is a matter of opening your heart and inviting someone else to come in for a visit. Just put yourself in their shoes, then write a poem for the you that's in those shoes."

The broken lady stared out the window, and seemed to be looking for something she knew she would not find out there. "I'm afraid my heart's not a place anyone else would want to visit. Not anymore."

Maggie leaned forward, resting her forearms across her knees. "Yes. And that is precisely why you must invite them in. For both of you. See, you don't write the whole poem. You only write half of it. The reader writes the other half. You give the gift, and the gift comes back to you."

The broken lady opened the pink journal to a place past the middle and looked into the blank pages. "You gave so much, Maggie, to me and everyone else. But I really don't have anything to give."

"You don't understand, Carrie Anne. Not yet. But you will. Poetry is like healing. Healing is not something you give. It's something you share. You write a poem to invite someone else to share in your pain, and thus in your healing. Then you share in theirs. The poem isn't whole until you give it away. It's a paradox, isn't it, that you can only freely give that which you don't possess." I could see that the broken lady was crying, and it struck me as being another paradox that healing so often begins with tears. "The real miracle," Maggie went on, "isn't in the love you give to someone, it's in the love you draw out of them."

"They're all one, you know," Maggie said softly. She turned her head and looked up at me, hiding in my corner on the ceiling, and winked. Then she turned back to the broken lady in her wheelchair. "Sharing means both giving and receiving, both at the same time. Hurting and healing are one, just different points on the journey. Like looking at snowflakes in a silver bowl, you can never tell where the hurting ends and the healing begins."

The broken lady was alone now. Like the transition from hurting to healing, I couldn't really tell the exact moment when the broken lady and I again became one. I was simply back in my wheelchair, with Maggie's pink journal in my lap. It was my hand moving the pen, but I knew that I was only the medium through which Maggie was writing her farewell poem.

> And when I die
>
> I want to die
>
> like a firefly
>
> on the windshield…
>
> An exploding efflorescence of Soul
>
> …Escaping

ALL OVER AGAIN

If I had it to do all over again

And did it all over again

I'd still be here again

Wishing once again

I had it to do all over again

All over once again

C.A.M.

Chapter Twenty-Four

"East or west? Should I go to Duke or Stanford?" It had been almost three years since Dr. Paulson had told Robbie that he'd make a good doctor, and now he'd been accepted to his two top choices for pre-med.

Robbie was talking about college. I was thinking about Mark and Maggie. No, actually I was thinking about loss. Mark and Maggie were gone, and now Robbie was getting ready to leave. But then I realized that what I was really thinking about was loneliness. I'd finally gotten adjusted to my new life in the house Robbie had worked so hard to make wheelchair-accessible, and now he was getting ready to leave. And then I saw that under it all, I was really thinking about myself. Once again, despite my best efforts to rise above myself, when the last peel of the onion fell away, there was my own Self right smack at the core. How can you lose yourself to find yourself if your Self always finds a way to insinuate itself right back into the center of yourself? "How do you answer a question like that?"

The look on Robbie's face told me that, without meaning to, I'd said the words out loud. "I don't know, Mom. That's why I asked you."

"I'm sorry, Robbie, I guess I was sort of daydreaming."

"Imagine that," Robbie said with a chuckle.

"Imagine that," I echoed. I had a memory flash of Andy Brennan telling me how Job's healing process had started when he stopped thinking about his own problems, and instead prayed for his friends. Perhaps, I thought, you find yourself by losing yourself in the quest to help others find themselves. Or at least in helping your son figure out where he should go to college.

I pulled a yellow pad from the pouch on the side of my wheelchair and laid it on my lap. Then I drew a straight line across the top, and a vertical line down the center of the page, forming a big letter T. At the top of the page, in block letters, I printed the word "Duke" and underlined it twice. "Remember what Dad used to do when he had to make a difficult decision?"

"You mean the T-off?"

"Yes. Why don't we do a T-off for the pluses and minuses of each coast?" As I was speaking, I wrote the words "plus" and "minus" on the left- and right-hand sides of the T. "Let's start with Duke. What are the pluses? And leave out basketball. If you're going to be a doctor, you won't have time for that."

"There's always time for basketball," Robbie said with a nod and a smile, "so put that down first in the plus column." The T-off took the better part of the afternoon. When we'd finished, I handed both sheets of paper to Robbie, one for Duke and one for Stanford. He studied the pages for a while, going back and forth between the two. Then he folded them up and put them into his shirt pocket.

"Mr. Foreman," I asked, "has the jury reached a verdict?"

"We have, your honor," he replied solemnly.

"Will you please share that verdict with the court?"

"Yes, ma'am, I will." Robbie stood up, took a deep breath, then belted out *California Here We Come!* as he danced around the room. Stanford had won.

That evening, I made a cup of hot chocolate and parked my wheelchair on the back porch. It had become my late summer evening ritual, watching the afternoon fade away while waiting for the fireflies to make their appearance. I was reading a book of McZen's Little Nuggets of Wisdom that Maggie had left me: *What Is the Sound of One Hand Praying?* Turning a page, I read:

The Lord works

In mysterious ways

And usually without

A sense of urgency

Setting the book down on my lap, I thought about the strange journey of life. Had it not been for that devastating accident, I would not have become a poetry therapist. Robbie might not have set his sights on becoming a doctor. Andy Brennan had been right. The path would unfold slowly, often torturously, and you would never see more than a step or two ahead. But if you just kept walking, why, you just might walk yourself right into a miracle. Or two.

One by one, the fireflies began to claim their place in the backyard firmament. In ancient cultures, they might have been seen as luminous souls of the departed. One by one, Mark, then Maggie, now Robbie – the three people I had most depended upon – had left me. And now, like fireflies in a meadow, one by one, new questions were intruding upon my consciousness.

When the mosquitoes started coming out in force, I wheeled myself back into the kitchen and reheated my hot chocolate in the microwave. As I waited for the chime, I opened McZen's book to a random page, which Maggie had told me was the best way to read a book of poetry, because that way you'd never finish it. It was surprising, really, how often these poets seemed to be speaking directly to me through whatever poem I happened to chance upon. Here's what McZen had to say as the fireflies danced into the embers of evening:

> If you don't have a question
>
> You don't have a clue
>
> If you aren't searching
>
> You must really be lost

McZen was right. The questions would never end. You just keep graduating to new questions. Bigger questions. Questions where the answers became more and more elusive. And the journey goes on.

THE DEAD POETESS SOCIETY*

How's the water, Virginia?

   Is that fur coat keeping you warm out there in the cold river?

Need another hand on the oar, Anne?

   Someone to help with that awful rowing toward God?

Whatchya cooking in the bell jar, Sylvia?

   A hollow wedding cake? Poppies in October?

Need another pill or two to help you stay asleep, Sara?

   Something to awaken new dreams in the burning moonlight?

Those old geezer poets sit around on their fat duffs waiting

For God to roll out the red carpet and invite them to come up –

And they get a movie made in their honor.

We poetesses smash down heaven's door, barge right in

Make ourselves at home –

And they call us crazy.

Poets Virginia Woolf, Anne Sexton, Sylvia Plath, and Sara Teasdale each took their own lives – they are still waiting for a movie to be made about The Dead Poetess Society

C.A.M.

Chapter Twenty Five

It was a perfect day for a dedication. And for two funerals. We were dedicating the Memorial Hospital healing garden, but inevitably, the replanting of the healing tree on the little island in the spot that Jerry Landerall had left for "just the right tree" took me back to the funerals for Mark and Maggie – funerals I'd missed because both times I was in a hospital bed. Over the past three years, Jerry's magic had transformed the healing tree from a dying stump less than three feet tall into a strapping 12-foot sapling that already cast enough shade to shelter a family picnic. And today we were putting her in the ground.

Robbie was sitting in the folding chair next to me, reading over his notes. He'd been asked to say a few words about Maggie later in the program, when they unveiled a plaque commemorating her contributions to the soul of the hospital. For me, it was another salted ice cream moment, bitter and sweet. I couldn't have been more proud of my son, who every day reminded me even more of his father. And who in a little over a month would be leaving for California to begin his pre-med studies at Stanford University, leaving me an empty-nester who still had broken wings.

Since taking Maggie's place as the hospital's poetry therapist two years earlier, I'd found myself not only writing verse, but also thinking in verse. Trying to be as inconspicuous as possible, I retrieved the latest pink journal from the pouch on my wheelchair and scribbled a few notes for a poem about how

Robbie the son was a reflection of Mark the father, and yet was also becoming his own man.

> There was a man in the rearview mirror
> I thought I'd lost him
> Disappearing into the distance
> But now I see him again up ahead
> Through a rain-spattered windshield
> Running toward the horizon

Pat Franklin, the CEO whose vision it was to create sanctuaries like the Healing Garden around the hospital, was speaking but I was hardly listening to him. Instead, I was sedating the butterflies by visualizing myself propelling my wheelchair up the ramp to the stage and then speaking to the hundred-some friends and dignitaries arrayed in folding chairs around the garden. And reading them a poem. I missed Mark sorely and would have given almost anything to have my legs back, but still (though the realization evolved slowly) the accident had brought blessings in its wake. One of them, I smiled to think, was that my knees could no longer shake.

"This garden represents our commitment to healing for the whole person." Pat looked up from his notes and scanned the audience, including a reassuring nod in my direction, probably imperceptible to anyone but me. "True healing recognizes not only our physical needs, but also our emotional and spiritual needs. It's not enough for us to cure the body, important as that is. We must also care for the soul." Pat went on to recount some of the things the hospital had done, and was planning to do, for what he called the softer side of a healing environment. I went on visualizing strength flowing into my arms so I wouldn't humiliate myself by rolling backwards down that ramp after being introduced.

"Let me say one more thing before we bring up Carrie Anne Murphy, our poetry therapist." Hearing the CEO say my name instantly woke up all those barely-sedated butterflies. "It's probably not something you'd expect a CEO to say, but our patients aren't the only ones who are in need of healing. It's all of us. I am painfully aware of the pain our people must leave in the parking lot every day when they come to work. Family problems, financial difficulties, emotional stress – these things demand care every bit as much as a broken leg or a virus. That's why we are redoubling our commitment to care for each other. Earlier, you heard our chief nurse executive Donna Westfall ask, 'who cares for the caregiver?' Well, the answer to that question has to be us. All of us. That's why I've asked Carrie Anne to expand our successful poetry therapy program to bring in staff as well as patients."

With one ear I heard Pat reading my introduction. With the other, I listened for the whisper of Maggie's voice reminding me that I could do this. "I've heard it said that you manage with prose," Pat said as he waved me to come up onto the stage, "but you lead with poetry. We're lucky to have our own resident poet here at Memorial, and she's helping all of us serve as better leaders." As Pat lowered the microphone to my level, I wheeled myself up the ramp. That morning, I'd told Pat that I'd make him the subject of the worst poem I'd ever written if he tried to help me up the ramp; this was a trip I had to make under my own power. Out of the corner of my eye, I saw Amanda give me a thumbs-up when I reached the stage.

Who ever would have thought that the journey which began in a high corner of the emergency trauma room would have brought me to this point? I adjusted the microphone and made sure that my notes were securely clipped to my dress so they wouldn't be gusted off. "I love what Patrick said about managing with prose and leading with poetry," I said, thankful for the opportunity to warm up to the audience before launching into my prepared remarks. "I think the same analogy applies in caring for patients. We *treat* people with prose – the notes we enter into their medical charts, the instructions we give them when they go home, the things we recommend they read in textbooks and on the internet. But we *heal* people with poetry. I don't mean that we all have to be poets – though I think we all do have a Poetry Muse hidden underneath whatever costume we happen to wear because it's expected of our job description. But there's a certain poetry of the soul, a lightness of the spirit, a spontaneity of the heart that lets us connect with people at not just a clinical level, but at a human level. Our dear friend Maggie Mermaid called it Jazz with Words, the improvisational spirit of a conversation in which no one has an agenda, but rather two people are riffing together. Like poetry, it's as much about listening as it is about speaking."

Jerry Landerall and one of the other groundskeepers were standing over on the bank of the pond, and the healing tree was sitting in the middle of the little rowboat that would transport her to her new home on the little island. At my request, Pat had agreed to have a delicately arched bridge built so that patients could walk, or wheel themselves, out to sit in the shade of her leaves – and had placed me on the design committee (when they put you on a committee, you know you've become a part of the hospital family). Acknowledging Jerry and his coworker, I began. "Maggie once told me there are two kinds of miracle – the miracles that happen to you and the miracles that happen within you. Memorial Hospital is a place that creates the kind of miracles that happen to you. Every day, medical miracles take place within the walls of this place. Some of us here today, including me, have been beneficiaries of these miracles."

A gaggle of sparrows set off a ruckus in the maple tree, and I smiled at the notion of writing Pat a memo-in-verse suggesting that he bring those boring budget meetings out into the healing garden, where at least we'd have some entertainment on the side. Then I continued my impromptu opening remarks. "But the miracles that happen within you are less likely to occur in the operating rooms and treatment rooms inside than they are out here in the healing garden, or in the chapel, or in the other places where – lonely and in pain – we ask the most important questions, the ones that almost by definition don't have good answers. Sometimes the miracle is simply accepting that no-good-answer is *the* answer. That there is no inherent meaning in your trials, there is only the meaning you create."

Jerry and his coworker had started to row the healing tree across the pond. "While we as healthcare professionals cannot bring about that second type of miracle, the one that happens within you, we can, and we should, create an environment that is more conducive to the happening of those miracles. As Pat mentioned, part of that commitment is the visible environment, as reflected in this healing garden. I want to talk about the invisible environment."

The sparrows took noisy leave of their maple tree and a surreal silence descended upon the healing garden. I smiled at the conceit that now I even had the attention of God. "The formula for spiritual health is the same as the formula for physical health. Avoid things that are harmful, and do things that are beneficial. It's just that simple. Simple, though not always easy. One of the poems Maggie shared with me early in my hospital stay was about turning every complaint into either a blessing or a solution. Now, instead of being bitter about being paralyzed, I'm grateful for living at a time when so much can be done for paraplegics. And I'm privileged to be part of the effort to find new ways that we can do a better job of making this hospital, and our world, more accessible to people with physical limitations."

I had not cleared my speech with the CEO, nor had he asked me to, but I was still apprehensive about the challenge I was going to issue to my hospital colleagues. *Proceed until apprehended.* I heard the whispered voice of Nurse Evelyn in the back of my head. I proceeded. "Maggie was right. I've come to realize just how emotionally toxic complaining is – not just for those who do the complaining, but for everyone around them. Many years ago, we made this a smoke-free hospital. We did this for the *physical* health of our patients and our employees. For the same reason, I challenge us to eliminate the emotional toxicity that is so harmful to our *spiritual* health."

I paused to read my audience. So far, so good. "It's been said that pain is mandatory, but misery is optional. As I sit in this wheelchair, I tell you that truer words were never spoken. There is, of course, a lot of pain in our hospital, and as Pat mentioned, it's not only our patients. But there's also a lot of misery, much of it petty misery, so petty we don't even notice it unless we're paying attention. All that petty misery accumulates, and it affects our ability to be the best caregivers we can be, to be the best parents we can be. The sad thing is, most of that misery is self-inflicted. And it is unnecessary."

I took a sip of water from the bottle that I always kept on the side of the wheelchair and smiled at another mini-blessing: a wheelchair is handy for hauling around a daily supply of groceries. Then I continued. "What if I could wave a magic wand and for one month erase all the emotional toxicity in this hospital, the way we once eliminated toxic cigarette smoke? Instead of whining about how far away they had to park, people would thank God they had legs to enjoy the walk in from the parking lot. Instead of moaning about the food, they would give Pat suggestions for how the cafeteria could make more money selling the sort of food they like... I guarantee he would listen." Pat nodded his emphatic agreement, earning laughter and scattered requests for swordfish, tacos, and Krispy Kreme doughnuts. "And instead of complaining about the patient in Bed 238, they would imagine themselves in that bed, and give the kind of care that they would want to receive themselves."

At this point, I departed again from my prepared remarks. "That was my room. I spent so many months in Bed 238 that I almost put roots down into the mattress. You know, our patients can tell right away who really cares and who's just going through the motions for a paycheck. And I'll tell you this. You can't be what Maggie called a bitter pickle-sucker out in the corridor (I made a face like someone who'd been born with a dill pickle stuck in her mouth and earned another laugh) and somehow transform yourself into a genuinely compassionate caregiver when you walk into a patient's room. Patients see right through the fraud."

I surveyed the audience, then returned to my planned speech. "What do you think would happen at the end of that month, the first time someone started to whine about the parking, moan about the food, or complain about the patients?" No answers. I continued. "I'll tell you what would happen. The same thing that would happen if someone were to light a cigarette today – they'd be shown to the next county." Everyone laughed, and no one louder than Bill Morton, the only member of the administrative team who still smoked.

"I challenge us to make Memorial the world's first misery-free hospital. That doesn't mean we won't have pain, it just means that we will no longer complain about our pain. We'll no longer inflict misery upon ourselves, and upon each other. It's a paradox that by refusing to allow the misery, we'll do a much better job of easing the pain. I learned that from a nurse right here at Memorial, the night she took a bit of extra time to read Emily Dickinson to me, and to tell me about Florence Nightingale." I waved to Evelyn Foster, who was seated in a folding chair parked next to the fountain, and she blushed. "Florence never complained," I continued, "and she had to endure a lot more than any of us ever do." Evelyn smiled and nodded enthusiastically.

"I know some of you are thinking it would take a miracle, and you're probably right, but one thing I've learned since becoming paralyzed is that miracles do happen. In fact, I now routinely expect them. And before you call me a Pollyanna, you should go back and read that story, or watch the movie, because that little girl Pollyanna, *despite* being paralyzed, did for her community precisely what I am prescribing for Memorial Hospital – she made a miracle happen. And we can too."

I looked down at Bill Terry, whose Indy 500 wheelchair was parked at the end of the front row, and saw him mouth the word "Amen," possibly referring to the fact that he'd finally taught me how to juggle. I blew him a kiss. *Where did that come from, Carrie Anne?* Nobody seemed to notice, so I must not have turned quite as red on the outside as I did on the inside. "Something else I've learned through my experience is that a healthy soul requires exercise every bit as much as a healthy body does. And poetry is a wonderful soul-building exercise. It's my pleasure to announce that over the next year, we will be inviting guest poets to give readings here at Memorial Hospital. We'll also be holding workshops for employees who would like to learn more about poetry as a means of self-exploration and self-expression."

I paused for a moment to reassure the butterflies, then retrieved the pink journal from the pouch on my wheelchair. "I'll close with a poem for the caregivers, and point out that we all have the opportunity to be caregivers, caring for each other. It's called Growing Soul." I took a deep breath, then commenced my first public poetry reading since the ninth grade.

GROWING SOUL

Take care of your garden, caregiver
Don't plant it with brambles and weeds
You won't grow orchids and roses
If in spring you plant dandelion seeds

Take care of your garden, caregiver
Nurture it with kindness and care
Help delicate buds become lovely flowers
With water and sunshine and prayer

Take care of your garden, caregiver
Protect it from bugs and from blight
Walk daily the rows with a vigilant eye
Shelter it from frost in the night

Take care of your garden, caregiver
Help that which was broken be whole
Then dance and sing as twilight falls round
Cultivate this home for your soul

I acknowledged the polite applause and closed the pink journal. "Way to go, Carrie Anne!" The raucous shout came from the far corner of the Healing Garden. Maggie was jumping up and down on the wooden bench, waving her arms like a cheerleader with pom-poms, wild red hair swinging rambunctious circles around her head. Nobody else seemed to see or hear her. I blinked hard, and when I reopened my eyes, Maggie had returned to the sea.

Chapter Twenty Six

"The most dangerous point in a newly-paralyzed person's life is not when they realize how badly they've been hurt; it's when they start to make real progress in their recovery. That's when they begin to appreciate just how long it's going to take, how hard it's going to be, and how limited their ultimate potential probably is. It's at that point they're most likely to become discouraged and depressed. I keep a very close eye on my patients at precisely the point where it seems like the worst is behind them. We've all worked too hard through a long and painful night only to lose everything just as the sun is coming up."

Amanda's words came back to me full-force as I read the poem that Bryan Hammerman had written as his latest poetry assignment. He'd been paralyzed in a motorcycle accident almost a year ago, and had indeed made great progress. He'd recovered full use of his arms and hands. But he was increasingly discouraged that his progress had run into a brick wall at the beltline. I never knew which Bryan would show up at our support group meeting – the one showing off the barbed wire tattoo on his bicep or the one drowning in self-pity because his legs couldn't tread water. The last lines of his latest poem froze my heart:

> I can still move my finger.
> I can still pull a trigger.

It was 6:30 on Tuesday evening. I was in the conference room where the Para-Quad Support Group would be gathering at 7:00. Bryan had agreed to meet me there at 6:00. He hadn't shown up. Nobody was answering the phone at his apartment. I was on the narrow cusp that separates merely worried from truly frantic. Bryan perfectly fit Amanda's profile of a high suicide risk: a young man who one minute has the world at his fingertips and an unlimited future at his feet, and a minute later – after flying over the handlebars of a motorcycle, diving from the top of a bridge, or tackling another football player – faces the prospect of life in a wheelchair. At 6:37 Bryan wheeled himself into the room. "Sorry I'm late. I had to check something out."

"No problem," I replied, trying my best not to sound like a distraught mom whose boy had just come home hours after his curfew. "What were you checking out?"

The chairs had been removed from around the conference table for our group. Bryan parked his wheelchair on the other side and laid a folder on the table. "My homework," he said as he slid it over to me.

"Thank you. What were you checking out?"

Bryan closed his eyes and puckered his face. "When the radiologist showed me the x-rays after the accident, he said there was no way I'd ever walk again, that I was paralyzed and would just have to deal with it." He shifted his weight in the wheelchair, looked down at his feet, then back at me. "Today..." He smiled like a kid who'd just stepped through the gates to Disneyland. "Today I wiggled my big toe. So I guess I'm dealing with it, huh?"

You know, there just aren't enough different words in the English language to describe the act of crying. I cry at weddings and I cry at funerals. And I cry when a young man whose hope had been taken away from him wiggles his big toe.

Caleb Johnson, the hospital social worker who specializes in working with people who have spinal cord injuries, facilitated our group. "Is everything okay?" he asked when he came into the room and saw me in tears. I nodded, but before Caleb could question me, other members began filing in.

As always, we began the meeting by going around the room, with each group member having the opportunity to share something, read the poem that was always my closing assignment for the next meeting, or take a pass. The way seating was arranged, it happened that Bryan would go first and I would go last. Caleb gave Bryan a nod. "Last week, you expressed your anger at people who have legs but don't use them. Any new thoughts you'd like to share this evening?"

At the previous meeting, Bryan had gone off on a rant about obese people who drive around shopping mall parking lots trying to find a space closest to the front door, waddle to the nearest escalator, then go in and stuff their fat faces with the all the fast food they can eat (Bryan's words, not mine). "People who abuse their bodies like that don't deserve to have legs," he'd said, "when I would give anything to be able to run up a flight of stairs or climb a tree." Most of that meeting had been focused on trying to help Bryan (and through him, the rest of us) transform his anger at the outer world into energy to tame the inner world. Caleb obviously wanted us to pick up tonight where we'd left off last week.

Bryan just smiled and shrugged. "I wiggled my big toe."

For a moment there was a stunned sort of silence in the room. *Did he say he juggled his yo-yo? He jiggled in deep snow?* Then the room was filled with clapping and a round of the awkward sort of hugs that people in wheelchairs give one another. It took Caleb ten minutes to get things back on track. When he finally did, he asked Bryan to say more about his feelings, and about what this meant to him, now that he could wiggle his big toe.

"I really haven't sorted it all out yet," Bryan replied. "At first I was really excited, you know. I'd have done back flips if I still could. But then..." He closed his eyes and bit his lower lip. Part of Caleb's genius as a group facilitator was knowing when to press the conversation and when to keep his mouth shut. He kept his mouth shut. We all filled the silence in our own ways – watching Bryan, watching anything but Bryan – but in our own ways we were sending him the power of our prayers.

"This is going to be really hard," he finally said. "You all know me. I'm not a patient guy – I can't even stand to wait in line at McDonald's!" Everyone laughed; you didn't have to know Bryan for more than about five minutes to appreciate that he didn't just have attention deficit disorder – he had what he called the RBADD version – Really Bad!

"Well," he continued, "last week I didn't have anything to wait for because I didn't have any hope of something worth waiting for. I was going to spend my life in a wheelchair. Period. End of story. But now, I can wiggle my big toe." He pushed his wheelchair away from the table and looked down at his feet, then pulled himself back in. "Does that mean that someday I'll walk again? Or does it just mean that today I can wiggle my big toe? It's going to be a long time before I know, and the uncertainty is killing me."

I must have frowned at Bryan without meaning to, because he immediately smiled and said, "Okay, Carrie Anne keeps telling us to be careful about the words we choose. The uncertainty really isn't killing me, it just feels like it. I want to know right now – will I walk again? I want to know if I'll ever stroll along the beach, feeling the sand between my toes and holding hands with my girlfriend. The uncertainty is torture."

"The problem with instant gratification is that it takes too long," Greta Faber interjected. She was one of the group's founding members, and could always be counted upon to inject a little note of humor at just the right moment. And usually to follow up with a gem of wisdom, as she did tonight. "Remember what Herr Rilke told his young poet friend. You have to train your doubt. Instead of letting it torture you, you have to teach your doubt to ask good questions. Instead of 'will I ever walk again?' teach your doubt to ask questions like 'what can I do to improve my odds of walking again?' or 'how can I make the most of my life if it turns out I never do walk again?' That's how you train your doubt."

We continued around the room, with each member sharing their thoughts on the torture of doubt and the power of hope. I tried to listen with half an ear, but mostly I concentrated on what I was writing in the pink journal. When it was finally my turn Caleb said, "Carrie Anne, you've been awful busy over there. Have you created something to share with the rest of us?"

I nodded. I'd long since stopped being shy or apologetic about reading unpolished poems that were written straight from the heart. "I've been thinking about the paradox that the miracle of healing often requires an incredible sense of urgency, and at the same time unbelievable patience. Both at once." I turned toward Bryan and spoke directly to him. "You need to work on strengthening that big toe, and getting the toe next to it to wiggle, with the urgency of putting out a fire. But you also need to leave walking on the beach with your girlfriend in the hands of God, and trust that whatever happens will be for the best. That's what this poem is about." I took a slow breath and silently recited my prayer. Then I read:

WAITING

I am patient
As nighttime peering toward the eastern sky
As an acorn sensing the fertile ground
As low tide feeling for the pull of the moon
Silence answers: not now but soon

I am patient
As an eaglet knocking on the door of her shell
As a sleeping bear on a thawing day
As a lioness brooding over unfed cubs
Silence answers: it's on the way

I am patient

As ocean surf pounding the sandy shore

As a mountain stream racing down bouldered slopes

As an August fire roaring through prairie grass

Silence answers: just a bit more

I am patient

As lightning on a summer night

As a funnel cloud dropped from a low black sky

As a hole dug six feet deep in the ground

Silence answers: you better slow down

"There's only one real finish line in life," I said after I'd closed the pink journal, "and you want to make lots of detours before you reach it. That six-foot hole is waiting for all of us, Bryan. Don't be in too big a hurry to get there. Now more than ever you need to remember that little nugget of wisdom from McZen – if you're not enjoying the journey, the destination will be a disappointment."

Chapter Twenty Seven

What do you write into a poem for a woman who no longer feels like a woman? I wadded up yet another page from my yellow pad and pitched it in the general direction of the wastebasket, missing by a car length. Thus far, I hadn't scratched out anything worthy of being entered into the pink journal, even as a draft, much less to be presented to Carol Mullins tomorrow afternoon.

I'd fallen into a pattern of writing poems for my patients while sitting in Mark's favorite easy chair in the den (not only was it the most comfortable spot in the house, I could tell Amanda that I got a workout every time I climbed in and out of it from my wheelchair). Chewing on the end of my pen, I contemplated the picture of snow-capped Mount Iliamna, a photograph Mark had taken from a kayak when we'd vacationed in Alaska. It was beautiful, it was forbidding. Like the challenge, and the privilege, of writing a poem for a woman who had lost her breasts, and then lost her hair, in the fight to save her life.

I scribbled a few lines to the effect that if God covered a volcano with snow, it didn't make it any the less a volcano, that its volcanoness was held in the fiery rumblings deep inside, not in the decorative smoky plume an artist would have us see coming from out the top. But the more I tried to draw the metaphorical bridge between volcanoness and womanness, the more trite and banal my poem became.

After an hour of littering the floor with yellow poet droppings, I finally set aside the pen. What would Maggie have written? Maggie could always find words to give hope even if there was no hope. Maggie once told me that, though she regretted not having had more years to live and to write more poems, she was thankful for having had cancer. If it hadn't been for the disease, she'd said, she never would have given herself permission to become a poet. She would never have known what to say without first having been in the shoes, or in the wheelchairs, of the people for whom she was writing.

What would Maggie have written? She would have written about how adversity is just part of the journey. That how we choose to deal with that adversity is what makes us become who we are in the process of our journey. She would have said that things which break you down can ultimately make you stronger. That's what Maggie would have told Carol. This is the part of the journey that requires strength. So be strong.

I closed my eyes and let myself drift into the wilderness of sleep. I dreamed I was hiking alone in the mountains. Walking through the pinewood forest, squirrels skittered about at my feet and songbirds celebrated the day in the branches, which sheltered us from the furious winds howling higher up the mountainside. I wanted to stay forever in this arboreal womb, but something impelled me upward. As I climbed, the trail grew steep and rocky; pine trees gave way to stunted shrubs. I had to crawl on hands and knees into the teeth of the relentless gale barreling down the slope.

As I continued to climb, the wind pelted me with sleet and snow. The force of the gale tore away my clothing. Wretched and freezing, I pulled myself across the ground, hanging on to each rocky handhold with the desperation of a drowning person clutching at thin air. Screeching like Satan, the wind ripped out my hair by the roots. The rocks tore into my hands and my knees, and still I crawled on, trying to ignore the pain. In one murderous gust, the wind pried open my mouth and yanked out my teeth, and in the next, gouged out my eyes.

Frantic now, I blindly clawed my way onward, hand over hand, having lost my legs to the cleaving of razor sharp stones. My screams for help were sucked out of my lungs before they could even take shape in my mouth. I was at the end of my strength, at the end of the world. I let go my grasp of the last stone anchor and waited for the gale to blow me off the mountain all the way to hell. Instead, a warm and loving hand lifted me from the wreckage of my body. "Welcome home," said a voice that was neither male nor female, yet somehow both. In that instant I knew that though I'd lost everything in the climb, I'd gained everything in the ascent.

The warmth of that loving hand remained with me in those drowsy moments when you can't tell whether it's dawn or evening, whether you're asleep or awake, or even which is your real and natural state. I luxuriated in the fuzzy glow until it had completely evaporated. Then it was time to get back to work. I had an appointment to keep. Maggie had been so right. Perhaps I could not give Carol Mullins hope, or healing, but I could share with her my own hope, my own healing.

Back in my wheelchair, I lit the spice candles on my desk and turned off the overhead light. I said my prayer, then opened the pink journal. After writing several drafts in the journal, I pulled out my calligraphy pen set and some deluxe parchment paper. It took the better part of the evening to get it right, but I finally got it right.

ABOVE THE TREE LINE

Shocking white clouds scream so loud against the sapphire sky
You have to squeeze your eyes tight to

Keep them from being pushed
    up against the wall
        at the back of your head.

Patches of summer snow remind you how fast
  the weather can change
    above the tree line.

How the sun can shine even as the sleet flies and the clouds
Fling white lethal fingers down to earth
And the thunder is so close it
Detonates scarlet explosions between your ears.

Above the tree line life is fragile, life is efficient.
Little goes to waste because there is little to go around.
It is stark, it is beautiful, it is unforgiving of the careless traveler.

Don't be afraid to touch me above the tree line
Where the earth makes love to the sky.

I'd made a sufficient number of circuits from coma to consciousness, from anesthesia to awareness, to know that there is a huge gray area in between the waking and sleeping worlds. This *not-yes* and *not-no* space betwixt these separate realities is the seedbed for miracles; it's where the impossible dream of today takes root, and becomes hope for the miraculous new world of tomorrow. I sealed this new poem into an envelope and prayed that as Carol Mullins traveled above the tree line, she would discover the meaning in her difficult journey, and that from that frigid bare peak she would, indeed, see the world as through the eyes of God.

THE GREAT DIVIDE

Clocks run faster on the distant side
    of the Great Divide;
and you never know when the sun might decide
    to set itself down without fair warning.
On the distant side of the Great Divide
    killing time is a capital crime.

Space contracts on the distant side
    of the Great Divide;
there's less room for error so you'd better
    get it right the first time.
On the distant side of the Great Divide
    wrong turns descend to precipitous dead ends.

The air is clear on the distant side
    of the Great Divide;
You begin to see the trail that leads to the place
    you are meant to be. Walk fast.
The distant side of the Great Divide might be
    closer than you think.

C.A.M.

Chapter Twenty Eight

"If you ain't scared, you ain't skiing!" The words were stenciled on the t-shirt of a deeply-tanned young man who didn't look like much of anything would scare him. I scribbled the phrase down in the pink journal, grist for a future poem. Nine years ago, Amanda had talked me out of an electric wheelchair. Now she'd talked me into joining her *Bum-Legged Ski Bums Club* on their annual spring trip to Lake Tahoe. Even better, Robbie and his wife Molly would be joining us. Robbie had just finished his third year of medical school at Stanford. Molly taught math at their local community college, but – and this was the best part!– she was taking a year off to care for their new baby Margaret Anne (who, we had already decided, would go by Maggie).

Before the accident, Mark and I had raced each other down double black diamond ski slopes. But nothing in my previous experience had come close to the terror, and the exhilaration, of having been strapped onto a ski-sled that was custom-designed for paraplegics, and set loose to fly down the bunny hill. By the end of the week, I was skiing down some of Tahoe's milder intermediate slopes. I knew I was skiing, because I was plenty scared!

The highlight of each day came in the afternoons, when I got to babysit little Maggie so Molly could ski with Robbie. We sat in front of the lodge fireplace, we two, I with my hot chocolate and Maggie with her pacifier, and I read poems to her. Classic and contemporary, she loved them all – even the ones I'd written.

Don't ask me how I know this, I just do, but her favorite was the one I completed right there, sitting in front of the fireplace with little Maggie on my lap:

OLD LADIES

I love watching people on their journeys
> Through airports.
Inventing make-up lives, romantic and mysterious,
> To match
The strange faces and costumes that skitter by like
> Exotic birds;

Especially the babies –
Babies on shoulders, babies on hips, babies in strollers;
Babies slapping the hard floors with their exuberant little feet;

Babies leading their parents on a merry chase down the
> Delicious new world of an airport concourse;
Babies running open-armed and wide-eyed to welcome their
> Beloved Grandmothers.

Grandmothers make us special.
Grandmothers make us human.
We're not just old ladies.
We're Grandmas!

One bleak day long ago, seemingly in another lifetime, I looked down from a high corner of a frantic room. I'd almost let those angels without wings in the bloody green scrubs lose the broken lady they were trying so hard to bring back. There were many days afterward that I'd wished I had let them lose her. Sitting in front of the fireplace with little Maggie, I knew why I'd come back.

MACGUFFIN

I've given my wheelchair a name
MacGuffin

The accident that brought MacGuffin
into my life

wasn't about being paralyzed
wasn't about being a widow
wasn't about being a poet

It was a slowly-emerging illumination
in a long conversation with God

A MacGuffin is "a particular event, object, factor, etc., initially presented as being of great significance to the story, but often having little actual importance for the plot as it develops" (Oxford English Dictionary).

C.A.M.

Chapter Twenty-Nine

In "Lady Lazarus," a poem from *Ariel*, the poetry collection that doubled as her elegant suicide note, Sylvia Plath wrote that dying is an art, like everything else. Ever since Maggie had died more than thirty years ago, I'd been working hard to develop my art of poetry. Soon it would be time for me to learn this new art. The other volunteers had all gone home so, as I often did these days, I draped a heavy shawl over my shoulders and wheeled myself out into the healing garden. When I was on the design committee, I'd made sure that the arched bridge out to the healing tree's little island wasn't too arched for a wheelchair, though of late it seemed to have become a bit steeper. This time, I had to stop at the crest for a moment to catch my breath. Then I wheeled myself over and parked next to the healing tree to watch the coming of night.

It was an enchanted sunset. Silver clouds stretched backlit arms across a blazing orange sky that looked like the furrowed field of a great celestial farmer. Out on the pond, the sun's rays transformed the rippled water into an ivory dance floor for glittering angels pirouetting across the surface. As the sun drifted below the horizon, it threw out a spray of gold that would be a proper crown for the maker of the universe. I wondered how many times the sun had set on this spot since the creation of the world, and how many more times it would set again before the world's end. *What was before the beginning of time? What happens after she writes her last rhyme?* Still, I knew this particular sunset was unique, a special display for me alone.

I stretched my arms wide the way I imagined Moses must have commanded the Red Sea to part so his people could pass and commanded time to stand still so I could live forever in this one moment. The tears come so instantaneously these days, I thought, as the skyscape went soft and blurry at the memory of Maggie – and all the other friends I'd made during my years as a poetry therapist. This evening was so peaceful, so perfect. And silent. The silence where the noise of man recedes and you can finally hear the soft insistent whisper of God. A silence so plentiful that you can take all you want and still leave behind all there is.

I sat by the healing tree as one might sit in audience with a revered teacher, slow and attentive, as if afraid to miss a single word that might enlighten me as to the meaning of life (that poem of Maggie's that I would never finish writing). Memories flooded back: the heartbreak of losing new friends only recently met, and the loneliness of being avoided by old friends who no longer saw me, saw only my wheelchair. Gradually, more pleasant memories surfaced. Maggie's practical jokes. Seeing Bryan Hammerman walk into the volunteer office with a cane in one hand and his girlfriend's hand in the other. The hours of sitting alone in the chapel praying for miracles and hoping at least for answers.

I hugged myself against the cold and shivered as the sky continued its nightly metamorphosis. Low over the horizon, against a backdrop as aquamarine as the Caribbean Sea, a new crescent moon reached its arms out longingly for the lovely Venus, forever hopeful but eternally denied. I recalled what Amanda the physical therapist had said to me so many years ago: "Whether you are cured or not will be in someone else's hands; whether you are healed or not will be in your own hands. Being cured is something done *to* you; being healed is something done *by* you. Ultimately, it's a decision, and a tough one. Being healed will be the hardest work you ever do. Paradoxically, the people who are most completely healed are sometimes those who have the least hope of being cured."

I tried counting the stars, taking notice of each new one as it popped into the firmament, but my mind wandered and I quickly gave up trying to keep track. As I drifted back and forth between dream and reality, I found it just as difficult to keep track of which state I was in. If only it were so easy to give up on *that* challenge, I thought, and give your life over to the worlds of your dreams. It was then that the healing tree reached her invisible arms around me, pulled me into the inner warmth of her trunk. No words were needed as we greeted each other, old comrades who over the years had shared so many hours, and written so many poems together.

"Are you ready?" she asked in a whisper more felt than heard. "No, not yet." I knew I was not audibly speaking – and that I didn't need to. Ever so gently, I felt my spirit rise above my body so I could look down upon the broken lady in her wheelchair by the side of the pond. "Have you forgiven everyone you need to forgive?" I gazed down upon myself, sitting alone in the wheelchair that had been my home for so many years. At that moment, I felt the last bitter core of a cold inner hardness soften. The malignant hatred I'd harbored all those years, that I had so many times tried to bury in the soil of the healing garden, drifted away like morning mist on a summer day.

"Yes," I whispered, "I can even forgive the man who killed my husband."

"There's more, isn't there?" the healing tree asked.

I felt myself melt back into my body. This time it would, I knew, be a short stay. A shooting star flashed across my field of vision, and just as instantly was gone. In ancient cultures more wise than ours, shooting stars were believed to be souls of the fallen, making their way to a heaven where every night they would grace the sky with their eternal pinpoints of light. I smiled at the thought of flying up to my new vantage point in the night sky, making friends with the neighboring stars. The healing tree was asking the question I'd been asking, and refusing to answer, for more than half a lifetime. Could I forgive God?

I reflected back on all the times I'd been angry at God, hated God, refused to believe in God. I wasn't resentful only for myself; even more so, I'd blamed God for taking the children, the little ones I'd grown to love so much during my years in the hospital – the children who would never grow up. I'd blamed God for taking the young parents who died way too soon and would never see their own children grow up, would never know the joy of being a grandparent. I'd blamed God for all the good people who would die so young when so many bad people were allowed to live for so long. I blamed God for taking Maggie, who in her whole life had never hurt a fly. Could I forgive God? *Awake I ask questions that are answered in dreams.*

The last wisps of sunset had given up their daily fight against the encroachment of darkness. I wrapped the shawl tighter around my shoulders. *What kind of a question is that, can I forgive God?* So many mysteries, so many unanswerable questions. Maggie's original pink journal, now showing its age, was, as it always was, in the pouch on the side of my wheelchair, but I didn't need to pull it out. I knew every poem by heart. And I knew the one I needed on this autumn evening. I'd never heard Maggie recite this particular poem – it was one of those she'd kept to herself – but tonight it was as if she was standing by my shoulder reading to me with a voice as clear as a mountain stream on a summer day.

Rhyme and Reason

I've climbed up in the mountains
To the foothills of the sky
Walked lonely through the desert
Seen great condors fly

I've played out in the meadows
With the flowers and the bees
Wandered through deep forests
And climbed high up in tall trees

Now I live with cancer
And soon I'll have to die
Then I'll go to Heaven
And know the reason why

I could see Maggie now, as clearly as a sunrise. Maggie, with her goofy smile, her baseball cap with the fake ponytail hanging out the back, the inimitable way she skipped when others walked, the angelic laugh that would have inspired Mozart to new heights of operatic genius. I didn't know why Maggie had to die, but at least now Maggie knew why. I also knew that it wouldn't be long before I would hear Maggie's joyous laugh again. Soon we would be together, and would read to each other poems of life and love, of mountains and heaven, of the meaning of life and the reasons for death. And soon I'd be in Mark's arms again.

The sun will shine tomorrow,
> though I might be sick in bed.

The sun will shine in a million years,
> though I might well be dead.

C.A.M.

Chapter Thirty

I was coming back to the healing garden for what I knew would be my last visit. Robbie had stopped by the volunteer office where the other old ladies and I were crocheting baby blankets. He was a doctor now, a practicing cardiologist at Memorial Hospital. I'd asked him to come by this evening and take me on a tour through the hospital, and then out to the healing garden. He pushed my wheelchair slowly through the hospital corridors, solicitous of the memories – painful and beautiful – that inhabited this place of healing, which for a deeply-etched fragment of time had been my home.

We paused for a long time at the hallway leading back into the oncology unit. Even after all these years, they'd maintained the framed display featuring some of Maggie's best poems, the Maggie-grams that had touched so many lives in the course of her own too-short life. I smiled at the picture of my little mermaid's impish face with the dazzling green eyes and the wild red hair that only I knew was the only thing about her that wasn't real.

A young hospital volunteer in a blue polo shirt held the door open for us. It was a lovely September evening, and a faintly exotic breeze drifted across the healing garden, inspiring the wind chimes to make their music. The healing tree – which had been no more than three feet high when Maggie first brought her into my room – now towered over the island in the center of the pond. Robbie pushed my wheelchair up to the water's edge and

I heard the long-familiar click of the wheels being locked. We sat in silence, Robbie's hands resting on my shoulders.

Something was moving out there under the tree, something vague and fuzzy. *These old eyes are playing tricks on me.* I shut my eyes and felt the breeze play across my face and sing softly in my ears. It was a familiar song, long unheard but never forgotten. *An angel in the window, a mermaid on a moonbeam.* When I opened my eyes again, the image under the tree had become more distinct. There was a girl on a swing. Her long red hair flowed wild in the wind, her emerald eyes twinkled.

The girl on the swing looked back over her shoulder at the man pushing her. A man I had not seen in almost half a century. The only man I had ever loved.

They were waiting for me.

I put my hands on the arms of the wheelchair and slowly pushed myself up. Like an old sailor standing on dry land after a long voyage, it took me a while to regain my balance. I rocked back and forth a few times, then took a tentative first step. Then another. Mark and Maggie encouraged me on. A few more steps.

Out on the pond, halfway toward the island, I looked back over my shoulder one last time. Robbie was still standing there, his hands on the shoulders of the lady who had once been broken. I smiled and waved, though I knew I'd stepped into a world my son could not yet see. Then, hand-in-hand with the man I'd always loved and the daughter I'd always longed for, I walked into forever.

Whenever you pass by the field where you have laid your ancestors
look well thereupon, and you shall see yourselves
and your children dancing hand in hand.

Kahlil Gibran, The Prophet

THE END

QUESTIONS FOR DISCUSSION

These questions will help you think about how the story in The Healing Tree can relate to your own life story. They will also give you ideas for discussing the book with friends and family, coworkers, and participants in a staff retreat, support group or book club.

Carrie Anne's is a fictional story, but in a larger sense it is also the story of millions of people who have transformed a shattering adversity into the platform for a future miracle. But people don't, and can't, bring about these transforming miracles without help – lots of help. What is our collective responsibility – within our families and within society – to help those who have suffered serious misfortune? What is our individual responsibility to devote some of our resources (time as well as money) to helping others?

Patrick Franklin, the CEO of Memorial Hospital, commented on the fact that there was a lot of pain in the organization, including the daily pain experienced by employees. He could have been speaking about any organization anywhere, couldn't he? Combining his comments with those of Pastor Andy Brennan, about how people who actively participate in support groups can heal more quickly, consider this question: what can any of us do to give our workplaces more of the qualities of a support group, in which members are there for each other, help each other, and when appropriate, pray for each other?

In her speech in the healing garden, Carrie Anne challenged her coworkers to make Memorial the world's first "misery-free hospital" by transforming every complaint into either a blessing or a solution. She acknowledged that this would probably take a miracle, but added that in the years since her accident she had grown to routinely expect miracles. Discuss the climate of your own workplace – how much toxic emotional negativity is there, and what is the impact on morale, productivity, and even people's health? What would it take to mount such a challenge in your organization?

At a time when Carrie Anne's dreams had been shattered, several people played key roles in helping her find new dreams – Maggie, Amanda, Evelyn, and others. What is our collective responsibility to help people find new dreams in the ashes of their nightmares, and what techniques can we use to do so?

The Gallup organization has conducted studies showing that many people have strengths that they are never called upon to use at work. This could include, for example, a nurse who likes to write poetry, which is not part of the nursing job description. Should managers encourage people to find a way to bring a strength to work? Should employees look for ways to see their job description as a floor – the basic requirements upon which they add their own special touch – rather than as a ceiling – limit on what they are willing or able to do on the job? How can we foster a workplace environment that encourages people to share their strengths rather than hide them?

In *The Healing Tree*, Dr. Paulson encourages Robbie to think about becoming a doctor. Yet in the world of today, many doctors are telling young people to avoid medicine because of the bureaucratic hindrances and income limitations. What is the responsibility of the professional (in any profession) to promote his or her profession, and/or to promote his or her organization?

Maggie told Carrie Anne that writing poems for others was as much a part of her own healing as it was of the healing of the person for whom she was writing. One of the principles of Alcoholics Anonymous is that of "mutuality." The relationship between the recovering alcoholic and his or her sponsor is a two-way street. *Being* a sponsor is as important for the recovery process as *having* a sponsor. How could adopting this philosophy of mutuality help any of us be more effective as parents, as managers, as coworkers, and as caregivers? Discuss how this philosophy pertains to your relationships – at home, at work, and in your community.

In introducing her poem *The Hope Diamond*, Maggie makes the distinction between false hope and true despair. In our roles as parents, as managers, and as caregivers, how do we make the judgment as to when to encourage people to pursue their "impossible" dreams, and when to tell them to face reality? How do we strike the best balance, for ourselves and for those we are seeking to help in their own journeys through life? In discussing this question, it is useful to consider the distinction between positive thinking and wishful thinking: *Positive thinking is expecting something and working to make it happen; wishful thinking is hoping for something and waiting for someone else to make it happen.*

At one point, Carrie Anne uses the term "protective denial." In his book *Blindsided*, Richard M. Cohen describes his experience in dealing with a devastating illness. He said that for him, "denial has been the linchpin of the determination to cope and to hope... Denial encourages anyone to test perceived limits and, as a consequence, to postpone concessions. There is nothing wrong with that." Do you agree, and if so, what is your responsibility to allow someone else to engage in "protective denial," even if you think they are being delusional?

For a long time, Carrie Anne rides on an emotional roller coaster. In poems like *Blue Ice* and *Resting in Peace*, she is in the pit of despair. Yet by story's end, Carrie Anne has started a new career as a poetry therapist, learned how to ski with special paraplegic equipment, and become a grandmother. How do people find the strength and the courage to stay on the roller coaster without falling off, and what can we do to help out when that roller coaster hits a downturn?

"Where was God? Why didn't God do something?" These are inevitable questions after any sort of tragedy. They are certainly questions that Carrie Anne asked (and which Andy Brennan did his best to answer). What do you think? Where was God in this story? Where is God any time that war, natural disaster, or other tragedy strikes?

In discussing her living will with her son Robbie, Carrie Anne draws a line between life in a wheelchair, which she was willing to live with and fight for, and life as a brain-diminished human vegetable being kept alive by machines. This is a hugely controversial issue in our world today, which has enormous implications for the allocation of limited medical resources, not to mention human health and dignity. Where should the line be drawn, why should it be drawn there, and what will it take to gain public support for drawing that line?

When Carrie Anne suggested that she would begin with an electric wheelchair, Amanda the physical therapist commented on how it would totally change the way others looked at her. To what extent has our society stigmatized people with disabilities, and what else can be done to remind all of us that these fellow human beings deserve to be treated with equal dignity?

What do you make of Bryan Hammerman's "rant" about obese people waddling into shopping malls to stuff their faces with fast food? What does it say about our culture of mindless self-indulgence, where obesity is a major health problem, gambling is a huge growth industry, shopping is what drives the economy, and debt is the fastest growing item on our collective balance sheet? What do the various dramas in *The Healing Tree* tell us about personal responsibility and accountability in our world today?

Thank God Ahead of Time is the title of a book by Father Michael Crosby. It is also an excellent mindset for dealing with adversity, real or apparent. Many people look back on adversity as having been a blessing, in the way that Bill Terry (the wheelchair juggler) did. What can *you* do to internalize the "Thank God Ahead of Time" philosophy yourself – before you need it? How can you help others do the same?

About the Author

*J*oe Tye is CEO and Head Coach of Values Coach, which provides consulting, training and coaching on values-based leadership and cultural transformation for hospital, corporate and association clients. Joe earned a masters degree in hospital administration from the University of Iowa and an MBA from the Stanford Graduate School of Business. He is the author or coauthor of twelve books. His latest book is *All Hands on Deck: 8 Essential Lessons for a Culture of Ownership*, a business parable with a crucial real-world message for today's organizations. Prior to founding Values Coach in 1994, Joe was chief operating officer for a large community teaching hospital. On the volunteer front, he was founding president of the Association of Air Medical Services and a leading activist fighting against unethical tobacco industry marketing practices. Joe and his wife Sally have two adult children. They live on a small farmstead in Iowa, and their second home is a tent in the Grand Canyon. He can be reached at Joe@JoeTye.com

ACKNOWLEDGMENTS

*A*t its best, there is an almost magical spiritual connection between caregiver and cared-for, a generous mutuality in which roles become blurred – like the reflection of snowflakes in a silver bowl, as Maggie said of the transition from hurting to healing. Though there are obviously too far too many people to call out by name, I want to begin by acknowledging the compassion of all the caregivers who really do care, and the pain of those who transcend their own suffering and help others along the healing journey, often within the community of a support group. God bless you all. Especially Sally Kletzky, whose courage and faith were such an inspiration to so many, and who now sits with Maggie in the shade of the celestial healing tree. (Sally, Maggie Bear still goes with me on every Grand Canyon hike.)

At Values Coach, Inc. we've been blessed to work with some wonderful hospitals, healthcare organizations, and professional associations. I hope that mentioning these executives will suffice for their whole teams, and apologize to those I have not mentioned by name: Alex Spector, Judy Rich, Les Donahue, Todd Linden, Steve Long, Patrick Charmel, Susan Frampton, Marty Fattig, Jeff Hill, Genny Maroc, Don Patterson, Mimi Roberson, Sharon Hays, Dave McClung, Mike Schneiders, Carol Wahl, Karen Crocker, Shawneen Buckley, Ed Lamb, Patsy Youngs, Fran Finley, Ryan Smith, Bonnie Nichols, Charlie Franz, Brian Hoefle, Leigh Cox, Frank Lazarro, Jeanne Locklear, Roger Looyenga, Jeff Harrold, Ron Simon, Jeff Stroburg, Sarah Dorman, Terrie Long, John Keelan, Karen Tinkham, Dr. Ray Troiano, Larry Schrage, Joyce Seward, Bethanne Kunz, Larry Schrage, Paul Cox, Susan Pendergrass, Susan Yeager, Dennis Smith, Kathleen Allman, Sandy Haryasz, Rand Wortman, and Dave Gilbreath.

As of this writing, more than 100 hospitals and other healthcare organizations have signed up for The Florence Challenge, though I hope that by the time you read the book thousands more will have made the commitment to promote a culture of ownership that is characterized by commitment, engagement, passion, initiative, stewardship, belonging, fellowship, and pride. These are essential qualities defined in *The Florence Prescription* – which is in many respects a companion book to *The Healing Tree*.

I am very grateful for the support and encouragement of the amazing team at the American Hospital Association, including Alden Solovy, Neil Jesuel, Laura Woodburn, Connie Lang, Dave Parlin, Patti Costello, Liz Summy, Kourtney Sproat, Mark Colluci, and the rest of the crew. Likewise, I appreciate the efforts of state hospital association executives and their staffs, including Jerry Jurena, Laura Redoutey, Kirk Norris, Beth Ingram, Becky Anthony, Art Spies, and Lara Hewitt.

Thanks to the meeting planners and speakers bureaus who help us share the Values Coach message, including Executive Speakers, The Tiller Group, Five Star Speakers, Health Forum Faculty, and in particular Tim Bateman at Lincoln Healthcare Events who gave the book a "Spark" at a key time.

I greatly appreciate our pioneer Certified Values Coach Trainers and Mentors, including John Roberts, Jeanne Locklear, Jolene Hoffman, and Vic Rosenbaum.

I am blessed to have an extraordinary team of dedicated colleagues at Value Coach, Inc. and could not begin to do my work without the support of Michelle Arduser, Thuy Do, Hung Viet Tran, Miss Bonkers, Tung Hoang, and Dick Schwab. Paula Yrigoyen and Jeanine Sedlacek have made valuable contributions to the organization, as have Chuck Lauer, Kurt and Mari Stocker, Elena Barabashova, Dave Altman, Dr. Ken Kizer, DeAnn Fitzgerald, and the other members of our Advisory Board.

Anyone who writes a book owes a debt to those writers who have been an influence and an inspiration. In particular, I have been influenced and inspired by the poetry of Billy Collins and by Steve Pressfield's essential book *The War of Art*.

A special tip of the that goes to the lovely and talented women who play Carrie Anne and Maggie in the movie.

Lisa Peterson and her team at Studio 6 Sense are responsible for the design of this beautiful book (our third such collaboration).

For Mom and Dad, it's true that the fruit falls not far from the tree, I'm a very fortunate fruit! Steven and Jackie, Nancy and David, Allen and Karla – I love you all, and all the brilliant nieces and nephews you've brought into the family.

Finally, this book is dedicated to Sally, Annie, and Doug. You are always in my heart and on my mind.

SPARK YOUR SUCCESS – 8 UNIQUE AUDIO CDs FOR BUILDING YOUR BUSINESS – AND FOR BUILDING A GREAT LIFE

Spark Your Success features 8 full-length audio CDs that will revo-lutionize the way you see yourself, galvanize you to change your attitudes and behaviors, and catalyze you to take the immediate and sustained action to help you transform your dreams into memories of the future.

CD #1: Get that Pickle Out of Your Mouth

How to have a more positive attitude and promote a more positive workplace.

CD #2: 12 Steps to Manage Anxiety

How to transform the paralyzing negativity of fear into catalyzing energy for action.

CD #3: Winning the War with Yourself

Using principles of military strategy to conquer YOWE (Your Own Worst Enemy).

CD #4: Actions You Can Take to Have More Energy

Energy is life, and this CD will show you how to have more of it.

CD #5: The Self-Empowerment Pledge

Seven Simple Promises that Will Change Your Life.

CD #6: Building on the Pyramid of Self-Belief

The four levels of self-belief, and how you can use them to build a better future.

CD #7: The Magic of Metaphorical Visualization

Revolutionary techniques to dream bigger dreams and make them real.

CD #8: The Janitor in Your Attic

An amazing motivational journey through your body to Spark you for Success, every day!

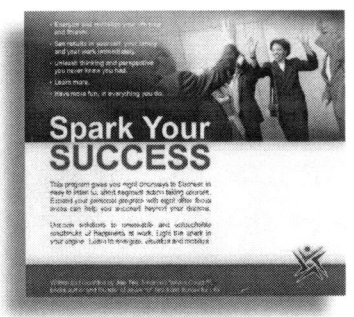

Order this and other great products at

www.SparkStore.com

or call Values Coach at

800-644-3889 (319-624-3889)

HAVE JOE TYE SHARE THE SPARK WITH YOUR GROUP

*J*oe Tye is CEO and Head Coach of Values Coach Inc., a company he founded in 1994. He is a dynamic, passionate and knowledgeable speaker who also knows that it takes "more than a pep rally" to change people's lives. He provides powerful and proven tools and techniques and then inspires people to put them to work in their businesses and in their lives. Here's just some of what you can expect from a keynote by Joe:

- Practical skills for courage and perseverance based on the ultimate success formula: *Never Fear, Never Quit*

- The power of words, questions, and stories to supercharge your business and transform your life

- How to stop cheating yourself by settling for anemic dreams and goals, and practical strategies for thinking big, dreaming big, and achieving big

- Ten strategies to cultivate a more positive attitude and foster a more productive team environment

- The Power of Values to build a culture of ownership and a commitment to excellence

Joe is author of twelve books, including *The Florence Prescription, Staying on Top When the World's Upside Down, Personal Best,* the international bestseller *Never Fear, Never Quit: A Story of Courage and Perseverance,* and his newest book, *All Hands on Deck: Essential Lessons for Building a Culture of Ownership — From Legendary Business Leaders Who Did.* He will challenge, he will inform and teach, and he will inspire and motivate you to dream big dreams and achieve big goals. He is the ideal opening or closing keynoter for your program – and will give your audience a toolbox of take-home resources, *because it takes more than a pep rally to spark a business and to transform a life*!

Attendee feedback and testimonials from Joe Tye's Programs

"Joe was an excellent, engaging presenter. He had a timely thought provoking message for our audience. The reviews from the attendees were outstanding! He provided captivating sessions motivating and demonstrating what we can achieve while making positive change."

— Judy Dahle, RN, MS, MSG
Education Coordinator, OR Manager, Inc

Attendee feedback from the OR Manager Conference on The Florence Prescription for Building a Culture of Ownership

Content Evaluation	Responses	Yes	No	%Yes	%No
Appropriate for your knowledge level	263	263	0	100	0
Relevant to your professional practice	263	262	1	100	0
Met personal objectives	261	260	1	100	0
Speaker Evaluation – Joe Tye					
Adequate Knowledge of subject	261	259	2	99	1
Delivered material effectively	259	258	1	100	0
Adequate time for questions	258	258	0	100	0

"Joe's message and presentation is so powerful that within 2 days, I have observed positive changes throughout the organization... The Florence Prescription has spread like wildflowers among our employees and the community, and the 8 banners give us a daily reminder of the culture of ownership that we are going to foster in our hospital."

—Patsy Youngs, President, Texas Health
Presbyterian Hospital Kaufman

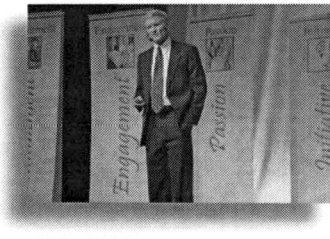

For information about booking Joe as a speaker, purchasing copies of books, and to sign up for his Spark Plug newsletter, call the Values Coach office at 800-644-3889 (319-624-3889) or contact Joe directly at joe@joetye.com

JOIN THE FLORENCE CHALLENGE AND HELP YOUR ORGANIZATION FOSTER A SPIRIT OF PARTNERSHIP AND A CULTURE OF OWNERSHIP

*A*t Values Coach, we believe cultural transformation begins with people making changes in their personal attitudes and behaviors. The three steps of The Florence Challenge will help your people be better parents, better workers, and better people. And that will help you be a better hospital. In taking The Florence Challenge, we are asking people to do these three things:

1: Read the Book

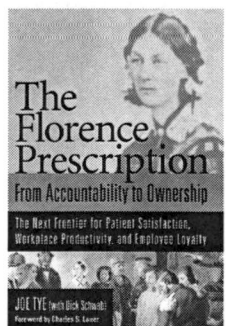

The Florence Prescription: From Accountability to Ownership is available as a free unabridged eBook at The Florence Challenge website, or can be purchased for just $5 each from the Values Coach office (800-644-3889). This is an engaging fictional story that has a very real-world message for hospitals, and the 8 essential characteristics for a culture of ownership help you create a shared vision for creating a great place to work that does a great job of compassionately caring for patients.

2: Take the Self-Empowerment Pledge

The Self-Empowerment Pledge contains 7 simple promises that change people's lives in every dimension – personally, professionally, financially, and spiritually. And if enough people at your hospital make a good faith effort to live these promises, you will better serve your patients and community, and your people will better support each other.

3: Join the Positivity Conspiracy

In *The Florence Prescription*, consultant Carol Jean Hawtrey calls upon hospitals to eradicate toxic emotional negativity (TEN) from the work environment the way we once eradicated toxic cigarette smoke. *The Pickle Challenge* is a fun yet effective way to make people more aware of the deleterious impact of TEN on themselves personally, and to help people hold each other accountable for positive attitudes and constructive behaviors.

There is no cost or obligation to participate in The Florence Challenge. It is our way of helping your people engage in the spirit of partnership that's essential to a meaningful experience of work and to providing the highest quality of patient-centered care.

To join The Florence Challenge or to request additional information call Values Coach:

800-644-3889

TheFlorenceChallenge.com

Values Coach, Inc.

Transforming People through the Power of Values

Transforming Organizations through the Power of People™

Jordan Creek Plaza, P.O. Box 490, Solon, IA 52333-0490

319-624-3889 • ValuesCoachInc.com